Deliverance and Inner Healing (and Restoration) in a Nutshell

How to Get Set Free

Straight from the Heart of God to Your Heart

Prayers Included

By Nancy Eskijian

Deliverance and Inner Healing (and Restoration) in a Nutshell

by Nancy L. Eskijian

Signalman Publishing
www.signalmanpublishing.com
email: info@signalmanpublishing.com
Kissimmee, Florida

ISBN: 978-1-940145-75-4 (paperback)

978-1-940145-76-1 (ebook)

Printed in the United States of America

If the Son therefore shall make you free, ye shall be free indeed.

—John 8:36

The Spirit of the Lord is upon me, because he hath anointed me to preach the gospel to the poor; he hath sent me to heal the broken-hearted, to preach deliverance to the captives, and recovering of sight to the blind, to set at liberty them that are bruised, To preach the acceptable year of the Lord.

—Luke 4:18-19

Dedicated to the Lord Jesus Christ, the Author
and Finisher of our faith.

CONTENTS

INTRODUCTION. 7

FIRST LEVEL: The Sin Issue—Repentance and Forgiveness. . .13

    Repentance. 13

    Forgiveness. 19

SECOND LEVEL: Demons. 32

THIRD LEVEL: Curses. 54

    Generational curses and patterns of sins. 54

    Curses from disobedience. 67

    Curses spoken from others. 77

    Witchcraft curses, spells, incantations and more. 83

    Personal curses. 88

FOURTH LEVEL: Soul Ties. 90

FIFTH LEVEL: The Inner Meditations of our Hearts: Attitudes, Vows, Negative Core Beliefs. 102

SIXTH LEVEL: Healing of the Heart. Deprivation, Loss, Legitimate Needs that are Unmet. 112

SEVENTH LEVEL: Dying to Self, and then, Walking in Newness of Life. 120

Appendix A: Prayers of Salvation, Repentance, and to Receive The Baptism of the Holy Spirit. 130

Appendix B: Unclean Spirits Mentioned in the Bible. 136

Appendix C: Prayer to Break Patterns of Sin in Family and Break Family Line Curses, Prayer for Breaking Control and Victimization

. . . . 139

Appendix D: Prayer for Breaking Soul Ties. 143

Appendix E: Renunciation of Sexual Sins. 144
    Prayers for Freedom from Sexual Sin
    Prayers to Break Ungodly Soul Ties
    Prayers to Break Curses of Sexual Sin

Appendix F: Warfare Prayers. 149

Appendix G: Understanding the Mother's Wound. 154

Appendix H: Understanding the Father's Wound. 158

INTRODUCTION

This book is a roadmap for your soul and a toolkit intended to give you guidance, revelation and power for freedom, healing and restoration. The Bible says in John 8: "[36] If the Son therefore shall make you free, ye shall be free indeed." The Bible also says in Luke 4:18-19 that Jesus also came to heal the brokenhearted and set the captives free. Jesus asked the paralyzed man at the pool of Bethesda, do you want to be made whole? John 5:6. That's an important question, because years of stagnation and disappointment erode a person's soul, as much as a person's body. We forget who and what we were supposed to be—we sit around and wait, instead of standing up and walking.

So that's my question to you today. Do you want to be made whole? I firmly believe God has the answer and is the Answer. Despite being born again, regular church attendance, prayer, counselling, reading the word, or even therapy and medication, believers still hurt and feel limited, perhaps there are trigger points of pain, anger, compulsive sin. You may ask, why am I repeating the failures of former years? Why do I still carry these negative feelings and patterns of behavior from the past? This book is here to reveal some answers to your questions. It's a fact we all need clarity and direction to obtain wholeness, and nothing is automatic. I am presenting a Biblical pattern backed up by the cross, the resurrection, and the word of God to help. Only God knows the depth of your heart and what you have been through,

I have been engaged in the ministry of deliverance and inner healing for many years. I believe that the Lord can heal and deliver in a multiplicity of ways. Gifts of healing(s) can be ministered to groups and individuals. Sometimes, there are prophetic words spoken that break years of pain and discouragement and give a new pattern of life and destiny. Often the gifts of the Holy Spirit work together for healing and freedom—discerning of spirits, prophecy, word of wisdom and knowledge, healings, working of miracles. Prayers of faith bring powerful results. God delivers many of us without human participation in ministry. Many times by just believing, obeying, and living we are set free.

However, in ministering deliverance and healing, I believe there can be a more deliberate and methodical understanding of the themes and patterns of bondage and hurt, and the processes of freedom and healing—of course, under the leading and power of the Holy Spirit and word of God. That is what this book is all about. The Holy Spirit is the Spirit of Truth, and the Holy Spirit is going take you on this journey, not me. The Holy Spirit is going to highlight in your soul and spirit what needs to be dealt with, and, in what order, as you read this book. The Holy Spirit is going to "trigger" you in good ways for your deliverance healing and restoration. I am going to define "deliverance" as freedom from demonic oppression, curses (generational and otherwise), judgments in the spirit realm against us, compulsive patterns of sin and failure, and breaking of ungodly soul ties. I am going to generally define "healing" as inner healing from traumas and hurts, even generationally, the pain of trespasses against us, self-inflicted wounds, and the events and losses of life, however caused. Included in the process is "restoration" where the Holy Spirit accelerates growth in areas that were blocked because of the foregoing, accelerates development and maturity, and restores and grows our souls to the dimensions God intends in our new and ongoing walk with the Lord. I am going to propose that God does many things on many levels at the same time and in many ways, and we have new revelations all the time that open the doors of freedom.

KEEP DIPPING: A short Bible story with a big message.

Maybe you know the story of Naaman (II Kings 5), the great Syrian military commander who had leprosy.[1] Naaman was not part of the God's covenant people; in fact he probably fought against Israel, but God allowed Naaman to experience a miracle, which convert-

---

1   1: a chronic infectious disease caused by a mycobacterium (*Mycobacterium leprae*) affecting especially the skin and peripheral nerves and characterized by the formation of nodules or macules that enlarge and spread accompanied by loss of sensation with eventual paralysis, wasting of muscle, and production of deformities —called also *Hansen's disease* 2: *a morally or spiritually harmful influence*

ed his heart. Naaman was a mighty warrior and had a position of wealth and honor in Syria, as the commander of the Syrian army, but even mighty and rich people can have big problems. Have you ever known anyone who had everything but was still a mess? In fact, you may even be doing well in some areas, but failing in others. So although Naaman was great, famous, powerful, and had money, he could not cure this disease. Winning on the battlefield didn't mean winning the battle of leprosy. Commanding men didn't translate into commanding a disease. God allowed him to be placed in a helpless situation so that His help could shine.

As the story goes, the servant girl of Naaman's wife, (someone who had been taken captive on a military campaign inside Israel), suggested that Naaman go see the prophet of Samaria, Elisha, because Elisha could heal him. Quite a bold statement for a servant girl! It was something that could have cost her life. After much confusion—contacts with the King of Israel, wherein Elisha finally intervenes in the political mess, the story unfolds to its victorious conclusion. This is not before there is a good deal of anger and pouting on Naaman's part. Naaman finally decided with the advice of some brave and caring servants, to follow Elisha's instruction. They tell him, if you had been asked to do a great thing, you would do it, but something simple has been presented to you: Go wash seven times in the Jordan River and your flesh will be restored to you and you will be clean. In point of fact, God doesn't want us to do a "great thing" on our own, we are asked to enter into the simplicity of trusting God's methods, be cleansed in the river of the Holy Spirit. Naaman argued that Syria had its own good rivers—but eventually agrees.

Now this book, in a nutshell, summarizes God's methods for freedom and healing. And isn't that what we are after? All through Naaman's story, pride is laid low, human methods are rejected, and humility motivated by desperation is required. We learn we cannot substitute our minds and methods for God's. We do have to humble ourselves for healing and restoration. Naaman didn't like going to the Jordan and washing seven times, he just wanted Elisha to wave his hand over him and set him free. That is a lot like our attitude towards freedom and prayer. Lord, just send someone to wave a hand over me (one-time prayer), and I will be great, and I can get on with my life. However, I have found, particularly in the area of inner healing and deliverance, that the Lord wants to teach us how we got where we are, and He wants to reach us in the innermost parts of our souls on an ongoing basis, and hopefully, to release us to help others once we understand the process of what it takes for freedom and healing. He gives us an understanding exactly how bondage occurs and how brokenness happens and what it takes to get on the other side of them. He is taking us out of a passive mindset so that we no longer accept the "abnormal," that is, a condition contrary to the will and word of God, as "normal," whether it is spiritual, emotional, or physical. He is launching us into a bigger perspective, despite our desire to clutch to our smaller perspective. That requires us to put our hearts and souls on the altar and open ourselves up for heart surgery. How did we get where we are? If we don't understand this, then the patterns and the processes are never understood and will be repeated. As an added bonus, once we understand who we are and how we got there, and how we can be free, healed and restored, we can help others. The dynamics of all relationships will change. Deliverance and inner healing expand our capacity to receive the love and truth of God, follow Him and become what God intended us to be.

When Naaman finally decided to go to the Jordan River and wash, (representing in scripture the cleansing of the Holy Spirit and starting a new life), he submitted himself to God, and then the healing began. There were a lot of good rivers around, but there was only one Jordan. Not only was he healed, but he experienced the True and Living God, leading to the conversion of his soul. We all must make that decision—take down the pride and anger, get humble and get into the flow of God's river of the Holy Spirit—the river that cleans and refines the innermost parts of our souls. Yes, there are good rivers, therapy, medication, learning how to deal with anger, general prayers, "bless such and such"—most of which are not particularly anointed, and that is the difference. It is the anointing that destroys the yoke of bondage. Isaiah 10:27. But there are some dirty rivers too, drugs, alcohol, sexual encounters and chasing money as a source of validation. Only the Jordan can make a true and lasting change. That's why Naaman could end up saying, "Behold, now I know that there is no God in all the earth, but in Israel." II Kings 5:15.

Please note as well, Elisha was not a professional physician who was accustomed to healing leprosy, he was a prophet of God, anointed by the Holy Spirit with the power to prophesy, heal, and do miracles. Likewise, believers, anointed by the same Holy Spirit, can be given the insight and authority to heal, set others free, and bring restoration. As you minister under the anointing, there will be a "quickening" in certain areas. The Holy Spirit is like a heat seeking missile, targeting key areas of pain, restarting growth or setting a person free.

I have known many people who desperately need help, but pride stopped them from receiving the blessing. Jeremiah said it so profoundly: Jeremiah 13: "¹⁷But if ye will not hear it, my soul shall weep in secret places for *your* pride; and mine eye shall weep sore, and run down with tears, because the LORD'S flock is carried away captive." This is God's agony with the whole world—will they receive the love of My Son or not? In theory a lot of people want holiness and wholeness. In practice it takes some humility, submission, breaking, trusting, and releasing our own thoughts and ways—and if they don't hear, they will be taken captive. Jeremiah was prophesying about God's people. As I wrote in one of my other books, people generally want what they don't need and need what they don't want.

It takes dying to self and processing pain that perhaps an individual has avoided for several years. Pain is a terrible prison. Sometimes it hurts so much that it hurts even more to release it. It takes coming out of denial, uncovering what we have hidden, mostly unconsciously, and undoing the works of the devil. Our quick fixes are tossed aside and God starts a deep and abiding work that may take a while. One layer seems to be gone, but then another layer of truth and pain emerge. However, in the process of <u>experiencing our experiences</u> with the Holy Spirit *this time*, [instead of just <u>us alone</u> experiencing the loss, rejection, sexual violation, hurt...] and then processing them through to a godly resolution, we grow, become mature and compassionate to the needs and problems of others. Also, we are experiencing our pain (pain that was most likely suppressed or denied) with the Great Comforter, not through our own methods of comfort, [fill in the blank]. God's own Spirit is in the process. We have the assurance that Jesus bore our griefs on the cross, so we don't have to bear them. We just need to release them and let the power of the blood of Jesus and the Holy Spirit work in our hearts. Furthermore, the entrance and intervention of the Holy Spirit in our experiences can literally resolve years of conflict and pain in seconds.

We have to want holiness as well as wholeness and take our lives to the cross, and both must be married together for the new person in Christ. Salvation, of course, is free—we cannot add or subtract from it. It is a finished work on the cross. But once saved, the word directs us to participate in receiving that deep cleansing and restoration that all souls need—that's also free, but requires us to get into the river. The reality is, God is a holy God. His holiness and righteousness is a divine standard on which He will not compromise. It is His nature and character. It is the holiness of God that is released to us by the power of the blood of Jesus, that enables the true wholeness to follow. I say true wholeness, because there are types of wholeness that can be achieved without God, but only by the blood of Jesus may the Holy Spirit enter the inner person in the deep essential way that combines the forgiveness of sins with restoration of the soul. 1 John 3:2 - 3 (NKJV) "²Beloved, now we are children of God; and it has not yet been revealed what we shall be, but we know that when He is revealed, we shall be like Him, for we shall see Him as He is. ³And everyone who has this hope in Him purifies himself, just as He is pure." Psalms 23: "³He restores my soul, He leads me in the paths of righteousness for His name's sake."

In considering the story of Naaman, the Lord showed me seven levels of cleansing, deliverance, and restoration for the soul. Yes, there is healing for the body, but I believe healing and deliverance for the soul is the healing and freedom required in the center of us. Proverbs 4: "²³ Keep thy heart with all diligence; for out of it are the issues of life."

First Level—The Sin Issue: Repentence and Forgiveness

1. Repentance

The first level of cleansing always addresses sin in our lives—I say this because this is what Jesus addressed first to introduce the kingdom of heaven. Jesus said it and John said it: "Repent, for the kingdom of heaven is at hand." Sin amounts to actions and thoughts and attitudes in violation of the law (and heart) of God. Jesus was clear that He included our thoughts and attitudes when He said in Matthew 15:19 – 20 (NKJV) "¹⁹For out of the heart proceed evil thoughts, murders, adulteries, fornications, thefts, false witness, blasphemies. ²⁰These are *the things* which defile a man, but to eat with unwashed hands does not defile a man." It is the natural fruit of a self-centered, rather than a Christ-centered life—at our very cores, our very hearts, attitudes, hurts, memories, selfishness. We are all natural born sinners, spiritually separated from God, and inclined to sin. Isaiah 53:6 (NLT) says, "⁶All of us have strayed away like sheep. We have left God's paths to follow our own. Yet the LORD laid on him the guilt and sins of us all." Everyone has strayed. In essence, we are challenged to accept the Lord's view of things—what's sinful, what's harmful, what's wasteful, what's disobedient, what is a nice distraction (wood, hay and stubble, dead works), what's in and what's out, what's up, what's down. If we don't accept this, then the healing and deliverance can't come. The (W)ord created everything, and the (W)ord saves us, and the (W)ord defines what is life, what is death, what is real, what is not, what is love, what is truth, what is you, and what is me.

That being said, it may take some healing and processing for people to even admit to some types of sin. Sometimes we are so broken or in pain, that the last thing we can do or want to do is face ourselves. Maybe it is not an overt act of "sin" so much, as attitudes, unbelief, unforgiveness, pride, hidden anger, wrong ways of thinking, and emotional patterns we have adopted like manipulation and control. So the Lord gently takes us off of imitation life support so we can recognize the truth and the Way, the Truth and the Life.

Realize that the holy nature of God and His character, His commands and principles, His healing power and loving presence, are what brings wholeness and deliverance ultimately. If someone uses drugs or alcohol and now has an addiction, there is a spiritual requirement for freedom. Yes, this is sinful, it is harming my body, it is destructive, it is ruining my finances and family and my very soul, my mind, will, and emotions. I am engaging in criminal or immoral behavior to support my drug use. The use of the drug or alcohol has altered my brain and body and I am addicted. However, simply calling it a "disease" without recognizing the moral or spiritual element of the problem will not ultimately bring a solution that would release a person from responsibility—first of all to use the substance to begin with, and continue its use; and second, to get help; and third, to exempt the person from seeking the spiritual roots of the problem and spiritual solutions to the problem. Further even if there is a genetic or generational (will talk about later) predisposition that causes vulnerability to use a substance leading to an addiction, and even if use of the drug or alcohol has now changed the addict's brain function and chemistry, somewhere, somehow, someone had to make a decision. We must admit: I have hurt myself and others and my relationship with God. Because I don't know God and I haven't sought God, I gone in a direction outside of His will and goodness for my life. This is very basic, but you see, very important. Lord, I repent, I am sorry, I can't get out of this on my own, it has taken over my body and my thoughts and emotions, my finances, and then go from there. At some point this will be required. These admissions and repentance open the door for God's healing and deliverance—which may be very different than the world's ways. This is not to put down the rehabilitation, medication, therapy, or self-determination that are used to overcome addiction—even with prayer, but again, this is a different platform for healing and deliverance. I have known believers who were miraculously delivered from the use of drugs and alcohol. While there is a value in different methodologies for relief, the Lord can actually set people free, and/or the Lord can infuse these methodologies with His power through His ways of deliverance, inner healing and restoration.

Or, I know my continual angry responses to life are wrong, as well as the anger in my heart, so I repent for my behavior and feelings. Then the Lord can also show us the origins of that anger, frustration, massive pain from others, neglect, abuse, injustice—the heart keeps its own calculations. I understand that sometimes those calculations are on such overload that we seek escape. However, we have to do our part and He can do His magnificent work. Again, there is a spiritual element to all of life: Our separation from God, His best for our lives, His purpose for our lives, and our separation from ourselves and others must be addressed. It is not that someone has just caught a cold; they have made a choice that either takes them closer or further away from God and true life. We see in the Bible many people getting set free and healed. That can be any believer. God is a transformational God. Our fellowship with Him and our experience of Him change our lives. Yet, even when we cannot directly face our sins, God will start to do a strengthening and healing work, so we can agree with His word.

Add to that all the damage of the generations, generational sins, traumas, losses, deprivations, just being born into this confused and conflicted world ruled by the prince of the power of the air who bends hearts and minds, and sets us on a course to hell, and we can see why Jesus had to take not only our sins, but curses, penalties and judgments, sorrows, wounds, sickness, death and self on the cross. I will get into all of this in detail. The essence of sin is words, thoughts, feelings, and actions, apart from God. We inherit the sin nature, first of all as humans, because of an inherent separation from God, and also, a disposition or vulnerability to some sins because of generational curses. The DNA of the seeds of sin is planted in us. As a result, we are carnally inclined (living through flesh, emotions, feelings, thoughts—see below). Romans 8:5-8 "5 For they that are after the flesh do mind the things of the flesh; but they that are after the Spirit the things of the Spirit. 6For to be carnally minded *is* death; but to be spiritually minded *is* life and peace. 7Because the carnal mind *is* enmity against God: for it is not subject to the law of God, neither indeed can be. 8So then they that are in the flesh cannot please God." The natural man is in opposition to

God, no matter how good. The carnal mind is on a downward spiral of death because there is no intervention of the Spirit of God, the Spirit of life in Christ Jesus. That term "carnal mind," let's just say in my definition, is being led of the desires of the flesh and a mental/emotional process of reasoning, thinking and feeling without the intervention of God, leading to a life based on the same.

Sin encompasses behavior, overt thought, attitudes that violate the law of God. Iniquities can be our predisposition, intentions, our condition of lawlessness, the moral bent behind the action, or a deed violating law and justice, and there are many nuances and definitions in scripture. Trespasses are our offenses and faults. Transgressions—a breach of the law of God. While the new birth through the Holy Spirit and the blood of Jesus, makes us spiritually alive in Christ renewing our relationship with the Father, our minds and emotional life and history must be renewed. Jesus said, by their fruits you will know them, but the fruits always go to the roots that are hidden. I am going to use the word "sin" to include iniquities and trespasses and anything else in violation of God's law for the following discussion.

Sin is deeper than our actions or even thoughts, sin is the bent of our natures without the transforming work of the cross and the power of the Holy Spirit in the new birth. Without Christ we cannot address our sins in the depth God requires. All of us, when we came to Jesus recognized we were sinners. Something was wrong. Something went wrong. But the depth of cleansing God desires will require new eyes and a new spirit. Without the new birth and the life of the Holy Spirit working within us, we cannot even see our sins. David cried, "Create in me a new heart O Lord and renew a right spirit within me." Psalms 51:10. Jesus came to put an axe to the root of the trees. He is radical, relational and revolutionary.

Sin must be addressed with repentance at the cross. Without recognizing the Lordship of Jesus Christ, we cannot move onto the next levels of wholeness. Without choosing to believe the Word of God and what God describes as the proper boundaries and attitudes of life, as described in His commandments, statutes, testimonies, and

His path of love, FIRST, there is no hope to be whole in the limitless life of faith that the Bible describes. We are not just talking about some major overt action, but let's say a grudge. It pleases us to hold onto it. Anger, it pleases us to continue with it. What about not forgiving, why should I forgive, and on and on.

The top level of cleansing is to deal with the sin issue in repentance, and this leads to the other levels. Dealing with the sin issue allows God to be God—God Himself, His statutes, His laws, His commandments, His divine definitions, order and rule. This is saying, wait a minute, something is wrong here, and the Holy Spirit will show us. If we don't pause and allow the Lord's correction here, we will be living out of a false life that will take over. There can be no deeper healing, deliverance or restoration without dealing with the sin issue. Deciding to pause and readjust to God's standards may be an adjustment of attitude, bitterness, pride, guilt, a grudge, a way of making money, a way of satisfying ourselves and a lifestyle apart from His word, or a type of pattern that is unproductive. Let's be realistic, most of what the Lord will address is our internal life. The "fruit" may be an obvious act towards another person, for example, or something spoken by us, but the "root" may be fear, bitterness, anger, hurt and so on. I will deal with generational patterns and curses later with regard to the "roots."

Now, that being said, God in His compassion and mercy, allows us to be overwhelmed with His love and mercy and healing many times, so that we have the strength to take a closer look at our own hearts—eventually. I realize that sometimes we are so broken, it is impossible or painful to do any kind of self-examination. The Lord overwhelms us with His love, and then we can start to live, inch by inch in His way. Anointed ministers led of the Holy Spirit perform open heart surgery. Words of wisdom and words of knowledge and discerning of spirits can be the soft wrecking balls of the fortresses of the enemy, for example. Every one of us has had times when we were basically on "life support" and He wooed us back to life. David wrote, "His gentleness has made me great." Psalms 85:13. The Holy Spirit abiding in us begins to give boundaries to our thoughts, actions, emotions. The Holy Spirit overrides our natural bent and is the Great Helper. The Lord does not "rough us up" in this process, though the conviction of the Holy Spirit is confrontational at times. The Lord provides a cushion of grace not only in joyous times, but in the healing and delivering times. His favor is upon us.

So when I talk about sin, it is not to shove something into our collective faces, but realize that a separation from God, true self and others has occurred, and some time, in some way, we are going to have to deal with it if we want to grow up into the maturity that God desires which will make our lives productive in the destiny He has designed for us.

The power of repentance opens the door for not only our forgiveness but release from other uncleanness. 1 John 1:7 (NKJV) "⁷But if we walk in the light as He is in the light, we have fellowship with one another, and the blood of Jesus Christ His Son cleanses us from all sin. ⁸If we say that we have no sin, we deceive ourselves, and the truth is not in us. ⁹If we confess our sins, He is faithful and just to forgive us *our* sins and to cleanse us from all unrighteousness. ¹⁰If we say that we have not sinned, we make Him a liar, and His word is not in us." Look, all people sin at times and deceive themselves into thinking they have not, and, therefore, all people are liars sometimes. But eventually if we listen to the Holy Spirit and have humble and contrite hearts, we will forsake sin—because something better is experienced by us, a new and living way. The power of the Spirit of life in Christ Jesus is elevating us above our old natures. Then the deeper cleansing can take place. So, I think that we can also conclude that forgiveness of sins leads to cleansing of all unrighteousness—a huge bonus. We don't know what is in our hearts. If we think we do, we are deceiving ourselves. Psalms 19:12-14 (NLT) "¹²How can I know all the sins lurking in my heart? Cleanse me from these hidden faults. ¹³Keep me from deliberate sins! Don't let them control me. Then I will be free of guilt and innocent of great sin. ¹⁴May the words of my mouth and the thoughts of my heart be pleasing to you, O LORD, my rock and my redeemer."

But let's say we are up to the whole process. The Bible talks about "the strongman." I suggest that there is a strong man in the flesh and a demonic strong man. I will get to this later, because we often think of the strongman as a demon, but it is not necessarily so. The strong man can be our own strong control over our lives or the false life or false identity through which we have lived so long that the true life is scared away and put back in a box; it can be false selves or personalities we have adopted which are not necessarily demonic, but control our actions and emotional life. But remember as I John 4:9 tells us that we live through Him. My direction here is simply <u>surrender</u>. Let God be God in us.

At the end of the book in Appendix A are several prayers for repentance that you can study and say to yourself and God, and another person if you want.

2. Forgiveness

Equally important are the steps of forgiveness we need to take with others, ourselves and even God, for often we hold ourselves in captivity because we have anger and resentment against the Lord— all the unanswered questions and distresses of our lives. There is great power in forgiveness because unforgiveness will surely cause a root of bitterness to spring up that will defile many—perhaps for generations. Hebrews 12:15. These roots of bitterness need to be cut off with other measures of healing and deliverance so that we can walk on level ground. Without forgiveness we are tied forever to the presumed source of our hurt. Sometimes when we minister deliverance we literally pull out the "roots of bitterness" in people's hearts. Roots of bitterness can grow because of neglect, abuse, rejection, family disputes, losses and other reasons. Therefore, be careful what is growing in your heart, and pull out the bitter roots when the Lord reveals them to you.

The power of forgiveness is vast. Jesus' first message to the disciples after the resurrection: John 20:19-23 "[19] Then the same day at evening, being the first *day* of the week, when the doors were shut where the disciples were assembled for fear of the Jews, came Jesus and stood in the midst, and said unto them, Peace *be* unto you" Jesus has just burst through the walls to be with His disciples in His resurrection body. He is in a heightened fusion of spirit and flesh—His body could literally go through walls and doors. God in His graciousness has overcome their barriers to be with His loved ones. Doesn't He do the same for us? Overcome our barriers to be with us? The disciples were huddled and afraid. He says peace be unto you. Jesus calms our hearts before He sends us on our way. "[20]And when he had so said, he showed unto them *his* hands and his side. Then were the disciples glad, when they saw the Lord. [21]Then said Jesus to them again, Peace *be* unto you: as *my* Father hath sent me, even so send I you."

And then He hands off His ministry to them. He shows them His hands and sides—He shows them that He is real and that He has suffered too, and that He has borne our suffering, and been brutally treated at the hands of other human beings. He shows them His places of pain, but there is no longer pain, just victory. And perhaps too, the message is that they will suffer or have suffered, but He has carried it, buried it, healed it, sealed it, and through it, brought us redemption and salvation. Whatever we go through, He has already been through. He is the Author and Finisher of our faith. Then when He has made Himself real to us, we have the courage and power to go forward. The disciples are commissioned by Jesus just as Jesus was commissioned by the Father, but as a priority He gives them a message on the forgiveness of sins.

John 20: "[22]And when he had said this, he breathed on *them*, and saith unto them, Receive ye the Holy Ghost: [23]Whose soever sins ye remit, they are remitted unto them; *and* whose soever *sins* ye retain, they are retained." New Living Translation: "[23]If you forgive anyone's sins, they are forgiven. If you refuse to forgive them, they are unforgiven." What an awesome power has been handed to us. The disciples were first given the power to forgive sins when they were first made alive, born again, by the Holy Spirit, and then fifty days after the resurrection, they were given the baptism of the Holy Spirit to go forth in power to do what Jesus did; heal the sick, cast out demons, perform miracles. Pentecost was the day for the first harvest to begin.

Perhaps they needed to forgive those who had trespassed against them, and obtain their own forgiveness, before they exercised the power to heal and deliver. Perhaps the Lord put things in this order so that they could release the power of the blood first, before they released the power of the Holy Spirit. Perhaps the Lord wants us to experience forgiveness before we exercise His power in greater measures. The indwelling presence of the Holy Spirit can only fully have His reign when we forgive and are forgiven.

The power to forgive sins releases the resources of heaven, just as unforgiveness cuts off the resources of heaven. Matthew 16:18-19 "[18] And I say also unto thee, That thou art Peter, and upon this rock I will build my church—[The rock of revelation of Jesus as the Son of God] and the gates of hell shall not prevail against it. [The gates of hell cannot prevail against a church cleansed by the blood, and the gates of hell have no foothold if there is forgiveness from sin. The gates of hell cannot prevail against a church founded on the Rock Jesus and the revelation of Jesus Christ.] [19] And I will give unto thee the keys of the kingdom of heaven and whatsoever thou shalt bind on earth shall be bound in heaven: and whatsoever thou shalt loose on earth shall be loosed in heaven." [What are the keys of the kingdom? We have the power to stop or release things, stopping ungodly powers, and releasing the word of God, the Spirit of God, angels, the will of God, in the material and spiritual world.]

Jesus has the keys of death and hell—Revelation 1:18, and the key of David, Isaiah 22:22. He can open doors that no man can shut and shut doors that no man can open, but everything in between He has given to the church. His keys are keys of sovereignty and of His divine position as judge. But our keys are pretty big keys as well—keys to open the kingdom of heaven on earth and stop the kingdom of hell. Who else is supposed to do it?

The central verse and heart of the Lord's Prayer is "Thy kingdom come, Thy will be done, on earth as it is in heaven." We have keys. We can bind and loose. We can bind demonic forces, we can loose the power of God. We can bind the word of God to people, we can loose them from demons. Our mouths can stop angels or release them. In such ways we can release in heaven what God wills on earth. These are the keys of the kingdom.

But we can also bind people up by not forgiving, and we can bind ourselves up by not forgiving. We can loose the resources of heaven and others by forgiving and loose ourselves by forgiving. If we hate, we are bound, if we fail to forgive we are bound. If we do not release our hurts, we are bound, and if we do not permit God to work in our lives we are bound. But if we forgive, we create the environment for love again, and the environment for reconciliation. Love opens the doors for blessings and life. You see, forgiveness and repentance are pathways of life, for the release of God's favor, blessings, destinies, healing, deliverance, protection and more, whether it is personal forgiveness and repentance, or generational, which I will cover later.

God starts the clock over again. Just as He has given a prophetic message in the days of the week, so that every day something new would happen, after a night, the dawn would come and we could have the chance of a new start. So it is with forgiveness, we can start all over again, when we repent, we start all over with God, ourselves, and others. When we forgive, we allow others to start all over again in our hearts and in the spirit, and if we don't forgive, we can't be forgiven either and start all over. Perhaps it is toughest to forgive ourselves, but we must. That is why a life or family, even a people or nation, that has a heart of forgiveness can flourish, there is always newness and starting over again, with the power of an open heart and imagination.

Many people tread water and don't know how to move forward, because there are places in their hearts that are still damaged and places where there needs to be forgiveness, and if the Holy Spirit reminds you from time to time, forgive again and then again, remember Jesus talked about seventy times seven. And if the Holy Spirit reminds you from time to time, repent if you need to, perhaps the Lord is taking you to a new level. And if there is still hurt when you think of a person you have forgiven, perhaps you need God's healing touch in that situation—breaking of soul ties, processing of pain, taking down defensive walls, getting free from demonic influence, and asking for a new heart to fill the gap. <u>Forgiveness does not heal the pain, but it does open the door for God's power to work His healing.</u> Without forgiveness the pain cannot be released, and the Lord cannot even the score. I have seen people miraculously released when they finally forgave someone who trespassed against them, and then they were set free from oppressing demons. Afterwards the healing can begin.

And if you block all of this off, you become a block, because you are worshipping hardness of heart. If you harden your heart, you will become a rock, but if you stand on the Rock, Jesus, and the power of the shed blood, then the gates of hell will not prevail against you or me.

How the score gets evened: The Lord's Prayer says, "forgive us our debts as we forgive our debtors." At the cross the offenders and offended can be released. The Bible says vengeance is mine, I will repay says the Lord. He will "even the score" with the offender—the person who did wrong. He can heal the brokenhearted. He can even the score with the offended—the person who is the victim. He will restore the years that the locust and cankerworm have eaten away through losses, traumas, and violation.[2] He can accelerate growth and blessings. He is the repairer of the breach. He can flood our hearts with His Spirit to overcome our losses, disobedience and waste, and overwhelm us with His newness. So, even the score in your own heart by forgiveness, and then let God even the score elsewhere. Usually if we try to even the score ourselves, we will create a bigger score to settle and a bigger mess. Forgiveness diffuses the accumulative and escalating anger and revenge of the world. It is

---

2   During the time of the prophet Joel, these represented progressive forces that were sent to destroy the nation. Joel 1:4 says, "That which the palmerworm hath left hath the locust eaten; and that which the locust hath left hath the cankerworm eaten; and that which the cankerworm hath left hath the caterpillar eaten." There was no escape. But God promised restoration after repentance. Joel 2:25 says, "And I will restore to you the years that the locust hath eaten, the cankerworm, and the caterpillar, and the palmerworm, my great army which I sent among you." I am going to shorten this to "locust and cankerworm."

the power of the cross. The cross is for the innocent and the guilty.

I believe the concept of "forgive us our debts as we forgive our debtors" is even bigger than just forgiveness of the sins of others. Sins and trespasses are actions or omissions that have caused damage or have been out of the will of God, but <u>debts are the accumulation</u> of results from the actions or omissions, all the losses, pains, damage that were created. Yes, there is a stack of debts that we can hold against others and they can hold against us. Because this person did this, I lost my business and missed that opportunity, and got depressed, took drugs, got sick, my family broke up, etc.... So, the scripture to me says, release it all. Release the original act, and release all the cumulative losses, and let the Lord even up the score. Let the Lord restore to you His purpose and design.

Next, forgiveness opens the door to healing. When we confess our faults to one another, we can be healed. James 5:14-16 (NLT) "[14]Are any among you sick? They should call for the elders of the church and have them pray over them, anointing them with oil in the name of the Lord. [15]And their prayer offered in faith will heal the sick, and the Lord will make them well. <u>And anyone who has committed sins will be forgiven. [16]Confess your sins to each other and pray for each other so that you may be healed.</u> The earnest prayer of a righteous person has great power and wonderful results." Healing flows from confession to each other. <u>I do NOT believe that all sickness, mental or physical, is due to un-confessed sin</u>, but the word does tell us to confess our sins and pray for each other to be healed. When Jesus died on the cross the rivers of blood for forgiveness and His broken body for healing merged together. His sacrifice was for the healing for traumas and pain that our bodies absorb because of what has been done to us and the healing of emotions and hearts as well. Bodies and minds absorb emotional pain, just as they store physical pain. So let things go, as the Lord shows you on one level, and the healing can be advanced on another.

The scripture describes a priority for the Lord's blessings in Psalms 103: "[1]Bless the LORD, O my soul: and all that is within me, *bless* his holy name. [Start with worship of <u>Who He is</u>.] [2]Bless the LORD, O my soul, and forget not all his benefits [Bless God for what He does]: ³Who forgives all thine iniquities [First benefit, forgiveness]; who healeth all thy diseases [Second benefit, healing]; ⁴Who redeems thy life from destruction [Third benefit, protection and redemption from a life of destruction]; who crowns thee with lovingkindness and tender mercies [Fourth benefit, blessings and affirmative mercies—abundance]; ⁵ Who satisfies thy mouth with good *things* [Fifth benefit, fullness of good things]; *so that* thy youth is renewed like the eagle's" [Sixth benefit, renewal of life and youth.] Surely there is a divine order here.

Forgiveness leads to blessings and happiness. Psalms 32: 1 – 5: "¹BLESSED (HAPPY, fortunate, to be envied) is he who has forgiveness of his transgression continually exercised upon him, whose sin is covered. ²Blessed (happy, fortunate, to be envied) is the man to whom the Lord imputes no iniquity and in whose spirit there is no deceit. ³When I kept silence [before I confessed], my bones wasted away through my groaning all the day long. ⁴For day and night Your hand [of displeasure] was heavy upon me; my moisture was turned into the drought of summer. Selah [pause, and calmly think of that]! ⁵I acknowledged my sin to You, and my iniquity I did not hide. I said, I will confess my transgressions to the Lord [continually unfolding the past till all is told]—then You [instantly] forgave me the guilt and iniquity of my sin." Notice that the man's bones were wasting away, dry, the moisture of his life was gone. It is a dry place to be separated from God. But when he acknowledged His sin, everything lifted. But when he unfolded his past to the Lord—an important point, for everything is a process, then the Lord forgave His guilt and iniquity. Blessed, fortunate, and to be envied are those whose sins are forgiven. The goodness of God is on us.

Third, the power of forgiveness brings reconciliation: Nothing can be joined together without repentance and forgiveness. Jesus asked forgiveness for His executioners. What if He had not? What if He had retained bitterness in His heart? What if He had not released all of us who put Him there? If He did not forgive from the cross, He would have nullified and cross and He could not be our Savior. Love would have failed. He would have failed on the cross. But love never fails, and it *surely love did not fail on the cross*—His sacrifice was the greatest act of love in the history of the world, which allows us all to start all over again with ourselves, God and others. God could not do anything less. That is complete, unparalleled, infinite love. God. We cannot help others unless we forgive them as well. Nor can we really help them without our own repentance. Forgiveness is the path of reconciliation. It doesn't mean that they deserve forgiveness, it doesn't mean that they won't do it again, it just means that the path of heaven is open for us and for them, and the rest belongs to human will. If we refuse to forgive and let the power of the Holy Spirit do a work in us, then we have cut off our own salvation (wholeness) and perhaps theirs too.

When we forgive we release others from the full penalty of the law that would come against them. If they continue in their sins, then they can experience that penalty, but there is something that has to be loosed in heaven so that there can be something loosed on earth. If we do not forgive, we will be bound with the same cords that others have bound us with and always tied to the person in that area of pain, injury, insult or harm.

Luke 23: "[34] Jesus said, "Father, forgive these people, because they don't know what they are doing." What did Jesus mean? He meant they didn't know the cost of crucifying the Son of God. They were ignorant of how truly terrifying it should be to touch the Holy One of God. They were ignorant of the deep destructive results and con-fusion they would reap for generations and millennia, and the deep hurt and cruelty they were inflicting. The people did not know the extent of their loss, rejection, or destruction. Jesus at the cross knew that they could not possibly grasp the magnitude of their hatred, ignorance and recklessness, and so He forgave them. It was so God-like, so divine. It is a level of love that only a person who knows the Living God can do. Only a person who experiences eternity and is certain of God can do this. When we look back at our lives and remember the destruction that others have inflicted, the highest form of love is to render love for evil. The Lord shows us to release people who hate and hurt us deliberately and ignorantly. When we release others, we release ourselves from the power of their sin. And then, some tragedies and violations are so terrible that all you can do is forgive, or just die emotionally and live in hatred.

Likewise, the only way <u>not</u> to waste pain and suffering is to forgive people and yourself. When we don't waste pain and suffering, it begins to have a purpose. Pain can be the turning point of purpose. It is a place of choice where we can either go backwards and live backwards, or go forwards with God. The Bible tells us to overcome evil with good. We can transcend pain and suffering by the power of God to find the paths of healing, understanding of who we truly are, learn to be like Jesus, and help others by what we learn as well. This is not overnight and it is a lifetime process.

Forgiveness has truth in it, it recognizes who did what. Only with truth in the inward parts, can we expect wholeness to come, because we must be honest with ourselves and others and God. So we repent and forgive. Many people minimize what was done to them—oh, it wasn't so bad compared to someone else. Or they repress it—push it down with anything, food, sex, entertainment, earning money, or distractions—go on with life. Likewise, they deny it—pretend it all didn't happen, adopt an outward persona that acts as if all is well. When there is deep trauma, different personalities may be adopted to separate oneself from painful experiences and navigate life. These are the coverings of lies, ways of blocking the truth, illusions and delusions, to protect oneself. No, we must say, this person did this or that, and it was wrong. I did this or that and it was wrong. Then further truth can come. Psalms 86:11 says: "Teach me thy way, O LORD; I will walk in thy truth: unite my heart to fear thy name." That unity of heart is the end result of repentance, forgiveness, deliverance, healing and restoration, which allows us to walk in His truth. But, in all honesty, it takes the power of the Holy Spirit to repent and forgive.

Matthew 18:21 - 35 (NLT) "[21]Then Peter came to him and asked, 'Lord, how often should I forgive someone who sins against me? Seven times?' [22]'No!' Jesus replied, 'seventy times seven!'" This is an interesting verse because seventy times seven is a lot of times. And, of course, it means that there is no limitation on Jesus' command of forgiveness. We might think, enough is enough! Or that's the last time! This is worse than anything else! But Jesus does not place limitations on forgiveness. It also shows us that forgiveness is usually not a one-time action. We pray the transgressor (person who did wrong), gets the picture, (or not), and goes a little deeper to deal with the root issues that cause them to sin. The sin is only the fruit; the problem is with the root. Unfortunately, in the meanwhile, everyone around them has to suffer. So pray that people get to the roots. It will make life simpler. But maybe they will never get there. However, we will change as we forgive and trust the Lord. The parable behind this involves a king who forgave a servant who owed him money, but that servant didn't offer the same forgiveness to a fellow servant who owed *him* money. When the king found out that the first servant had not released his fellow servant, he was angry. In the end both of them went to jail, having to pay their debt. In short, without forgiveness everyone gets imprisoned. [35]"That's what my heavenly Father will do to you if you refuse to forgive your brothers and sisters in your heart."

Fourth, the power of forgiveness brings prosperity—not exclusively prosperity of money—though it can include that, recognizing that there are a lot of rich, bitter, unhappy and lost people, but prosperity of soul, which can lead to prosperity in many areas. If you are seeking an area of prosperity in your life, then enter into forgiveness and repentance. God wants to bless us with His prosperity. But the word states in Proverbs 28:13 - 14 "[13]He that covers his sins shall not prosper: but whoso confesses and forsakes *them* shall have mercy. [14]Happy *is* the man that fears always: but he that hardens his heart shall fall into mischief." We cannot prosper in our purpose before God without forgiveness. We cannot prosper in our hearts without forgiveness. Free hearts alone can receive the fullness of God's blessings, favor, wisdom, direction, peace, rewards. And out of our hearts come all the issues of life. But if we confess and forsake our sins, in other words let them go, and leave them, because a lot of people confess sins and never forsake them, we will have mercy. God's heart becomes soft when our hearts become soft and humble. Hardness of heart is a result of the deceitfulness of sin.

Proverbs 28:14 (TMSG) "[14]A tenderhearted person lives a blessed life; a hardhearted person lives a hard life." By the way, we must trust in the power of God to forsake sin.

The power of forgiveness digs deep into our hearts, even the hidden faults. Let the words of our mouths and the meditations of our hearts be unified with Him. Otherwise we are hypocrites. The only thing that will do this is forgiveness and the power of love, making Jesus Lord over our thoughts and hearts.

Fifth, the power of forgiveness releases sonship, authority, and inheritance on us. Luke 15:17-21 (NLT) [17]"When he finally came to his senses, he said to himself, 'At home even the hired men have food enough to spare, and here I am, dying of hunger! [18]I will go home to my father and say, "'Father, I have sinned against both heaven and you, [19]and I am no longer worthy of being called your son. Please take me on as a hired man."'" [20]"So he returned home to his father. And while he was still a long distance away, his father saw him coming. Filled with love and compassion, he ran to his son, embraced him, and kissed him. [21]His son said to him, 'Father, I have sinned against both heaven and you, and I am no longer worthy of being called your son.'" Although the prodigal son had gone his own way, broken his father's heart, wasted his inheritance, when he repented and found his way back, he was given the status of sonship that he did not realize before. The Father's desire is that we understand that we are His children, but sometimes it takes a breaking and a brokenness to get there. When we come back home, and receive His forgiveness, we understand that we are His children, and that never changes. What we obtain is a new appreciation and love for the Father. He hasn't taken away our inheritance. In fact, our inheritance in Him is so vast we cannot truly lose it—if we want it. We are the ones who have walked away. The older brother who never left home was a prodigal son as well. Although he had been "good" and never disobeyed his father, he didn't know the heart of his father. He might as well have been in another country. Although he was in the father's house, he lived in the bondage of trying to be good and earning the father's love, whereas Christ, the unseen third brother, imparts His goodness to us through grace. The love is already given.

When we are freed by Christ, we are freed to obey, and not under bondage to do so.

He has torn and He will heal as well. Hosea 6:1–2 (NKJV) "¹Come, and let us return to the LORD; For He has torn, but He will heal us; He has stricken, but He will bind us up. ²After two days He will revive us; On the third day He will raise us up, That we may live in His sight." The promise of the resurrection is contained in these verses, but we must return to the Lord. Yes, He does tear us, but He will heal us, and there will be resurrected life following.

Sixth, the power of forgiveness is connected to answered prayer and miraculous prayer. Mark 11:22–25: "²²And Jesus answering said unto them, Have faith in God. ²³For verily I say unto you, That whosoever shall say unto this mountain, Be thou removed, and be thou cast into the sea; and shall not doubt in his heart, but shall believe that those things which he saith shall come to pass; he shall have whatsoever he saith. ²⁴Therefore I say unto you, What things so ever ye desire, when ye pray, believe that ye receive *them*, and ye shall have *them*. ²⁵And when ye stand praying, forgive, if ye have ought against any: that your Father also which is in heaven may forgive you your trespasses. ²⁶But if ye do not forgive, neither will your Father which is in heaven forgive your trespasses." Unforgiveness clouds our faith and the power of our prayers. If we do not forgive, we have already placed our feelings above God, so how can we prevail in other areas? Let's win the battle in ourselves and we will be free to have faith in other areas. Overcomers inherit all things. Forgiveness is the key.

Seventh, forgiveness is the road of expansion; expansion of our capacity to receive from God and others. It tears down the walls of separation between God, ourselves, and others. One way to expand love in our lives is forgiveness. Forgiveness is the first step to healing the wounds of the heart, it is the preparatory work to the healing power of the Holy Spirit. Forgiveness acknowledges that God is in charge of our lives and that we must model His character. Forgiveness is an act of faith and love too, but it is designed to release the power of God onto our broken places, and those of others. Forgiveness works increase, because it works togetherness. Two are better than one. There has to be the Lord and us to begin with. Brokenness and sin and hurt and violation separate people, and people who are separated in an ungodly way are not positioned to increase. We must extend God's mercy to others as Jesus has extended mercy to us, and all the way around. Extend mercy to yourself at the same time.

Forgiveness expands possibilities. Unforgiveness decreases possibilities because we cut off the ability of our hearts to breathe and love others and connect with the Lord. If we forgive everyone and ourselves, we have the power to love everyone and ourselves, and love is powerful—love created the universe, love created you, love sent Jesus to the cross and raised Him from the dead. Love released and releases the Holy Spirit and restores families and cities and nations. Forgiveness is an act of faith, a requirement of the kingdom. There is no progress without forgiveness and repentance. Repentance and forgiveness are incredible tools of faith which are used in conjunction with all the other processes and means of deliverance, healing and restoration described in this book.

When there is unforgiveness, we are turned over to the tormentors. Jesus explained that in His parable too. Where there is forgiveness there is freedom, Jesus explained that with His life, death and resurrection. I spent a lot of time on repentance and forgiveness because we must understand that these are incredibly powerful keys for entrance into the kingdom. With repentance you supply the truth and God supplies the grace. With forgiveness you supply the grace and God takes care of the truth. I don't want to pound you with this, but we are going to have to repent and forgive for the rest of our natural lives, so let it be a pattern in your spirit. In other words, I am saying "get used to it" in a totally productive eternally rewarding way.

SECOND LEVEL: DEMONS

Once we have dealt with the Lordship of Christ, recognizing the truth as He states it and love as He demonstrates it, through repentance and forgiveness, then we can move to another step of cleansing. The scripture says that Jesus came to undo the works of the devil. The modern Christian might ask, just what are the works of the devil? To answer that question, we simply look at Jesus' ministry. Jesus, by His ministry model, and the cross and resurrection, reversed, or "undid" the works of the devil by setting people free from demons, sickness, sadness, sin, spiritual ignorance, separation from God, spiritual darkness, death itself—all works of the devil, by the power of His blood and the Holy Spirit. As a result, we are set free from the power and penalties of sin, while the results of sin can be mitigated (made less severe or painful). Jesus forgave people of their sins and set them on their feet again so that they could be restored to a relationship with the Father. Then through His death and resurrection, He passed on this ministry of "undoing the works of the devil" to His body, the born again, Spirit-filled, Spirit-led church. *The blasphemous onslaught against God the Father, God the Son, and God Holy Spirit, three in One, and the terrible path of destruction against all of creation, especially mankind, which started in the throne room of heaven itself by a rebellious angelic outlaw Satan who exported his rebellion and destruction to earth, contaminating man and woman in the Garden of Eden, could be undone on a continuing basis through the blood of Jesus, the name of Jesus, the word of God, and the power of the Holy Spirit, by believers.* As part of that reversal, we see the second level of cleansing, namely freedom from demonic influence. If the Son therefore shall make you free, ye shall be free indeed. John 8:36.

Jesus set people free from the oppression, possession, and compulsion of demons. When we read the scriptures it is clear that Jesus spent close to a third of His ministry on deliverance from demons. Did these spirits suddenly disappear now that we live in a modern world? No. I would say there has been a multiplied influence of demons because of the breakdown of traditional forms of protection such as marriage and the family and traditional institutions, and an exponential increase in every conceivable unclean, demonic, destructive, and deceptive communication and activity in our society and around the world—which hardly sums it up. There aren't even words for it. Jesus started His ministry with these words recorded in Luke 4:18-19: "[18]The Spirit of the Lord is upon me, because he hath anointed me to preach the gospel to the poor; he hath sent me to heal the brokenhearted, to preach deliverance to the captives, and recovering of sight to the blind, to set at liberty them that are bruised, to preach the acceptable year of the Lord." His themes, were deliverance, freedom, healing and restoration.

We will never gain our place of freedom and power that God desires for us, if we are controlled or oppressed by unclean spirits. Our power is reduced in the spirit realm, even if we are saved. I am going to use the terms "unclean spirits," "evil spirits" or "demons" interchangeably.

First of all, let me start out by saying that I do not believe a Christian can be *possessed* by a demon or demons. To be possessed by a demon would deny the reality the we are possessed by the Lord Jesus Christ and have been delivered by the Father from the power of the darkness and translated into the kingdom of His Dear Son, (Colossians 1:13), when we gave our lives to Jesus Christ and were initially "born again." That choice is backed up by all the power of heaven and our spirits are made alive in Christ. Furthermore, our souls have been granted an expanded ability to choose again due the Spirit of God working in, and the restoration and freedom we receive in Christ. In short we now have the capacity to be Spirit led, rather than simply led by our souls and bodies. No, we cannot be possessed by a demon or demons, we are now bought and paid for by the powerful and redemptive blood of Jesus shed on the cross and placed on the mercy seat in heaven.

However, demons do not automatically lose influence or stop oppressing Christians just because we are "born again". Born again is just that—a start in growth (a baby) to come to the full stature

of Christ. When we are born again we have the Spirit of God and
the will of God in our hearts to assist with our deliverance and our
walk as believers. Believers need to understand that being "born
again" is not just asking Jesus into your heart, but starting life over
again, starting backwards with the new nature and the power of the
Holy Spirit and blood of Jesus to ultimately come to the full stature
that the Father designed for each person from the foundation of the
world. (Believers can and still do open the door for demons to influence, oppress, and exert control in their lives every day.) Remember
Naaman. When he finally emerged from the Jordan for the seventh
time, his skin was like a little baby's. Maybe this is an important
message too. The cleansing of deliverance and healing starts us all
over again, like a little baby. You are being carried forward on a new
foundation on the Rock, Christ, rather than an old foundation on self
and the generational patterns of your family line. To be free there
is an unraveling process in the individual spirit, soul and body and
this process is an ongoing that takes us back to day "one," actually
further.

I believe Christians can be "demonized" or that parts of their
souls and bodies can be influenced and controlled by demons. For
example—just to illustrate that spirits can afflict areas of our souls
or bodies, Luke 13:10-17 describes a woman bent over eighteen
years. She had bondage in a physical area. It doesn't say her mind
was in bondage, or that she had uncontrollable urges, or she was
incapable of singing or eating. No, it says that a spirit bent her over.
"[10]And he was teaching in one of the synagogues on the Sabbath.
[11] And, behold, there was a woman which had a spirit of infirmity eighteen years, [A SPIRIT, NOT JUST AN INFIRMITY OR A
SICKNESS] and was bowed together, and could in no wise lift up
herself. [COULDN'T HELP HERSELF FOR FREEDOM FROM
THIS DEMON]. [12]And when Jesus saw her, he called her to him,
and said unto her, Woman, thou art loosed from thine infirmity.
[POWER OF THE HOLY SPIRIT AND AUTHORITY OF JESUS
APPLIED] [13]And he laid his hands on her: and immediately she was
made straight, and glorified God. [14] And the ruler of the synagogue
answered with indignation, because that Jesus had healed on the

Sabbath day, and said unto the people, 'There are six days in which men ought to work: in them therefore come and be healed, and not on the Sabbath day.' [15] The Lord then answered him, and said, '*Thou* hypocrite, doth not each one of you on the Sabbath loose his ox or *his* ass from the stall, and lead *him* away to watering?' [16] 'And ought not this woman, being a daughter of Abraham [SHE WAS IN COVENANT BUT STILL BOWED OVER BY THE DEMON], whom Satan hath bound, lo, these eighteen years, be loosed from this bond on the Sabbath day?' [17] And when he had said these things, all his adversaries were ashamed: and all the people rejoiced for all the glorious things that were done by him."

Now, we are under a new covenant, not the covenant of the law of Moses, as this woman was. We are the body of Christ, enabled by the Holy Spirit to undo the works of the devil like Jesus did. At that time, it was going to take Jesus to cast out this demon, or someone in a priesthood office who understood their authority. But my point is, the spirit did not possess her but diminished her wholeness in a certain area. Today we are kings and priests and we have a position in heaven to take authority over demons. We have the blood of Jesus, the name of Jesus, the word of God and the power of the Holy Spirit operating in us. We have holiness, authority, power and direction. We can cast out demons, even demons <u>in ourselves</u>. The woman had a spirit and that crippled her body eighteen years. It took the power of God to set her free.

Jesus told His disciples in Mark 16:17, <u>these signs shall follow those that believe</u>—they shall cast out evil spirits. Was Jesus just joking here or giving a suggestion? Were believers operating in signs, wonders and miracles, limited to the narrow crowd of disciples that were filled with the Holy Spirit in the upper room, and then it all fizzled out when they died? Or, are we, as believers, to carry on the mission? Obviously, He was telling us about the supernatural power we would have because He was leaving this earth. We, the body of Christ, would carry on His work to the ends of the earth. The power was given to those who "believe." If you believe, you are included in the group. I John 4:17 says, "As He is, so are we in this world." That means we are like Him in this world, with His character and power. Go ye into all the world and preach the gospel to every creature. You will be empowered by the Holy Spirit and see signs following. The disciples couldn't even fulfill the great commission then due to limited technology and travel. It takes modern transportation and communication.

Jesus told us that the first sign would be casting out demons, and the second sign is that we would speak with new tongues. There is a reason for this order, first, we would have power over the enemy— the power structure had shifted because of the power of the blood of Jesus through the cross, and second, to speak in new tongues is clearly either a gift of the Holy Spirit or evidence of the infilling Holy Spirit because of the resurrection and the empowerment of the church. So the "signs" would be done by Holy Spirit power. Jesus was leaving. Who was going to carry on His work? We are, empowered by the Holy Spirit, acting in faith.

Back to deliverance: It should be noted that the layers of cleansing, deliverance, healing and restoration often overlap. Also, they are part of an ongoing process. So while freedom may be gained in one area, the Lord may then take us to another level for a deeper work. He may guide those who minister to release restoration, healing, and development of the soul or identity. I have called forth a person's soul or asked the Lord for a creative work in their identity, at the same time commanding a spirit to leave that has brought confusion. It is a mixed creative and liberating work. There is no linear (simple step-by-step) progression in the transformation of our lives. It is multi-dimensional and multi-directional, often all at once, layer by layer, as the Holy Spirit leads, and it is ongoing until we depart from this planet. However, demonic influence or control, or as some call it, "demonization," will need to be dealt with at one point or another or at several points. Perhaps other layers can be addressed next, such as generational curses, inner healing, breaking soul ties and more. Perhaps the Lord will direct us to birth the "new person" out or pray for the growth or development of the true person that has been hindered in bondage since childhood, and all this is happening while casting out an unclean spirit, or breaking a curse.

Eventually, we must deal with the oppression of evil spirits, and their entrance and expulsion. In short, how they got in and how they can be kicked out. The why: In general demons do not enter where they are not invited, or, in an alternative and as a larger statement, a door must open for a demon to enter, whether deliberately or not. Demonic influence often comes in because of sin. Sin opens the door. It may not be our own sin, but someone had to create a breach in the spirit to enable an unclean spirit to influence or exercise control in a person's life. Demons must always have legal grounds—whether it is personal sin, being sinned against, trauma, ignorance and openness, occult curses and practices, generational curses, and more, to oppress a part of our soul or body. The devil is a lawyer—a nasty, low down lawyer who wants to keep us in bondage. (I have nothing against lawyers, I am a lawyer as well as a pastor). But the point is, the devil is using legal grounds like a prosecutor—really accuser, (for example our sin), to keep us in captivity. You should be in prison! You cannot get free! You deserve to be miserable and chained up! You sinned, therefore I can torment you! The devil tempts us and then accuses us—it's an effective system he has used on us from the beginning and we fall for it, all the time. On the other hand, we have a lawyer too. Jesus is our Advocate, our defense attorney, with the Father, (I John 2:1), and on the basis of His blood, He pleads for all that He bought and paid for at the cross to be released to His loved ones: Forgiveness, healing, deliverance. He took the penalties of sin; He provides the freedom from the power of sin. Most people who do not know our beautiful loving Father, believe God is the prosecutor, but really it is the reverse. The Father did not send Jesus to condemn the world but save it. He sent Jesus to be our Advocate. Sadly, if we do not receive Jesus as our Advocate, we will be judged by the Father without the benefit of Jesus as our Mediator (or Go-between).

Let me give you a simple example of a spirit entering due to sin—but I will get into this a bit more in the next few pages. If one exposes oneself to pornography, it is very likely that a spirit of lust or perversion is going to enter the soul realm. Pretty soon, one's thought life is in the visual realm of sexual sin and it becomes very driven.

Demons are manipulating you at this point—it is beyond natural thinking, and there <u>can even be physiological changes.</u> <u>This is not a fight that can be won in the natural.</u> The groves in hearts, minds and souls become emotionally and chemically reinforced. Jesus was quite clear—out of the heart proceed evil thoughts, adulteries, fornications etc. He knew it was an internal matter. You don't have to be committing a physical act or trespass to sin. Jesus knew the imagination was the first point of formation for sin, and therefore, rightly declared the "heart" had to be transformed.

As another example, if a person is sexually abused as a child, not only may spirits be transferred from the abuser to the child, but also anger, hatred, self-hatred, rejection, depression, spirit of sadness or oppression can enter the wounded heart. The initial transference was unwanted, and came through someone else's sin. The other spirits came through the open door from the violation. Emotional brokenness occurs, blocked emotional development, ungodly soul ties, patterns of pain, generational curses can be passed on and more.

You see how "deliverance of the captives," "healing the brokenhearted" are a mandate for healing and deliverance for all of us. Jesus didn't want that woman in the synagogue to be bent over for eighteen years and He doesn't want us bent over either. Healing and deliverance work together like a two punch. When ministering deliverance on any subject, let's say fear, it is always valuable to back track to the source, then there can be repentance and forgiveness, as needed, breaking generational curses, as described later, breaking ungodly soul ties, and then casting out the spirits. If you don't do this, then you are likely dealing with the "fruit" and not the "root." <u>Not every problem is demonic, and not every solution is to cast out a demon,</u> but it is important to recognize this area of cleansing, so a deeper healing and restoration can occur. Discerning of spirits is important in this area of ministry—what spirit is operating. A demon enters a groove created by damage or sin or generational breaches. Take away the legal grounds and the demon must go too. I like to have people repent in the area where a spirit has been discerned (both personally and generationally), renounce the sin, (if it is a sin issue), then perhaps break soul ties and ungodly covenants. Then deliverance (casting out the spirit, binding it up and commanding it to leave) becomes much easier. Afterwards, pray for healing of the brokenness. This way, that harassing unclean spirit cannot enter again.

Sometimes we are not dealing with a personal sin issue, but the person has been sinned against. In such a case, forgiveness will open the door for deliverance and healing. I have dealt with many people who find it very difficult to forgive another person who has hurt them. Yet, when they do, the tormenting spirit leaves easily. Until this happens, there is legal grounds for the spirit to stay. Many miraculous things happen with forgiveness. You don't have to "feel" forgiveness, by the way, just do it by faith.

Sin is fueled by something, and at times, that is an unclean spirit operating in the unredeemed portion of our natures, and sin can be fueled by generational patterns and broken parts of our souls. Take away the fuel and obedience is much easier. Evil spirits grease the skids of sin, and that spirit is empowered by sin. I don't mean this just in the physical realm, such as lusting sexually or lusting after money, which is surely driven in nature. I mean that demons fuel the fallen nature or nature not fully realizing redemption. They can push people to fear, to rebel, to anger, perversion, hatred, abuse, and violence, to name a few areas—how else could people do so many destructive and insane activities? These spirits themselves are reinforced on by higher level spiritual powers as well. We are not wrestling against flesh and blood, but principalities and powers. The prince of the power of the air is "working in the children of disobedience," bending their thoughts and emotions and influencing behavior, according to the course of this world, whatever that is currently. See Ephesians 2:2. On the opposite side, the Holy Spirit enables the new nature to flourish and influences our behavior. Philippians 2:13 says that God works in us to will and do for His good pleasure. There are two spiritual kingdoms (and only two). You are going to pick one, whether you realize it or not. There is no neutrality (can't sit this one out), or rest in some general good "vibe." There is only the kingdom of God and the kingdom of the devil, and the kingdom of God is established on His holiness, and the love and truth of God as revealed in scripture, and the kingdom of the devil is established on his uncleanness, rebellion and lies. Because of the blood of Jesus, and only because of the blood of Jesus, can we enter into God's holy kingdom.

The scripture shows us clearly that spirits can enter in childhood. In fact, in my experience ministering deliverance, childhood is *THE prime time* of demonic access because of the innocence of children, the ignorance or neglect of their parents or caretakers, or their actual participation in the harm of children. The demonic transference or influence can come from and through the caretakers/parents. Spirits also can come as a "packaged deal" generationally, just by virtue of being born. They may be transferred through occult activities of parents/previous generations, and many other ways. As described in Matthew 15:22-27, a Syrophoenician woman came to Jesus with a demonized daughter. She was "crying at the top of her lungs," one translation says. Her daughter was cruelly harassed by a devil. The disciples said, just send her away. Jesus Himself told her that His mission was to the lost sheep of the house of Israel. He said it was not right to take the children's bread and give it to the dogs. But she persisted. She fell down and worshipped Him, stating with great shrewdness and humility that even the dogs eat of the "children's bread." So Jesus delivered her daughter of the demon, long distance.

We know the story. Jesus said great is your faith--be it unto you as you will, and here daughter was made whole. Note, she wasn't in the Abrahamic or Mosaic covenant and therefore she accessed her miracle by her own faith—pointing to the new Gentile world of believers on the horizon.

Jesus calls deliverance "the children's bread." It belongs to the children of God—not to the unbelieving world, for then Satan would be fighting against Satan. That's our bread. It is not just the milk of the word that nurtures us. It is not just the honey of the word that enlightens our eyes and sweetens our bitter spirits, or even the meat of the word for the mature believer. It is bread—it is something for us at all times to go with all meals, an integral part of the plan of redemption. It is part of the Bread of Life. A good parent knows their child's bread is precious, it is important, and without it they won't grow or the meal would not be complete, and you don't want someone else to eat it. The woman said that even the dogs eat of the crumbs that fall from the master's table. She would do anything because the only way this child could be set free was to be delivered of this demon by Jesus. No program, no special school, no medication or counselling would cut it, she needed deliverance; and the mother, who wasn't even of the house of Israel, knew it. Sometimes children are careless with their bread and let it fall to the ground. Let us not be careless with this bread that the Lord has provided for us and let it fall to the ground. Let us take this part of communion with Jesus, for this too is the Bread of Life.

On the other hands, the enemy feeds us the bread of lies. "E-V-I-L" is "L-I-V-E" backwards. Sometimes we eat this bad bread because we are sick and something is better than nothing, and sometimes we become sick because we eat this bad bread. But either way, the lies and the demonic realm that is opened through them, is meant to destroy. Jesus is the Bread of Life. He has come to feed the world the communion of His broken body and blood for complete healing, deliverance and restoration.

How about the father whose son was throwing himself into the fire and the water? Jesus asks the father, how long has your son been doing that. The father answers, since he was a child.

Mark 9: "[17] And one of the multitude answered and said, Master, I have brought unto thee my son, which hath a dumb spirit; [18] And wheresoever he taketh him, he teareth him: and he foameth, and gnasheth with his teeth, and pineth away: and I spake to thy disciples that they should cast him out; and they could not. [19] He answereth him, and saith, O faithless generation, how long shall I be with you? how long shall I suffer you? bring him unto me. [20] And they brought him unto him: and when he saw him, straightway the spirit tare him; and he fell on the ground, and wallowed foaming. [21] And he asked his father, How long is it ago since this came unto him? And he said, Of a child. [22] And ofttimes it hath cast him into the fire, and into the waters, to destroy him: but if thou canst do anything, have compassion on us, and help us. [23] Jesus said unto him, If thou canst believe, all things are possible to him that believeth." Please note all the *types* of destructive behavior caused by this demon.

The demons don't wait until a person is 18 and ask, "may I please come in?" And they don't play fair. They come to the vulnerable, they come to the infant, they are passed on through generations, they come through sexual, physical, emotional and verbal abuse to little children, they come when children are exposed to perverse and evil things. They come with neglect, rejection, and abandonment and whisper that you are unwanted and unloved. They come to people, especially young people, who are ignorant and open, and expose themselves to evil. They tempt the child to be stubborn and willful and oppose the good plans of God. No, the devil does not play fair and he is willing to take out a child and ruin that young one for the rest of their life. Jesus was very angry at those who spoiled the hearts and lives of children. Luke 17: "[1]Then said he unto the disciples, It is impossible but that offences will come: but woe unto him, through whom they come! [2]It were better for him that a millstone were hanged about his neck, and he cast into the sea, than that he should offend one of these little ones." Basically Jesus was saying, it would be better for the millstone to be around the neck of the offender, than the neck of little one who would be drowned in perversity, trauma, shame or sadness. But it happens every day. How the Father grieves. Coming back to life is so much more difficult with broken, frozen, traumatized and hardened hearts, and the old dead world is passed on from generation to generation.

If a young person engages in self-destructive behavior (like cutting themselves, taking drugs, promiscuity, high risk behaviors etc.), certainly there can be a demonic element involved involved in the behavior. Also, because of such choices, the door is further open to demons.

If the Holy Spirit isn't empowering us, the world, the flesh or the devil are—all of whom are very strong. But instead of giving us freedom, evil spirits keep us in bondage. Who rules us when we do something we don't want to do or can't help what we do? Is it only the flesh and mind? That is not to say that the flesh and the emotional realm are not powerful—the flesh is strong, flesh and blood are very strong, but at times we are dealing with evil spirits that reinforce fallen flesh and blood.

James 1:13 - 15 (NKJV) "[13]Let no one say when he is tempted, 'I am tempted by God'; for God cannot be tempted by evil, nor does He Himself tempt anyone. [14]But each one is tempted when he is drawn away by his own desires and enticed. [15]Then, when desire (thought life and imagination) has conceived, it gives birth to sin (overt act of sin); and sin, when it is full-grown, brings forth death."

Demons cannot be cast out without repentance first and/or a desire that they be expelled unless we are dealing with someone who lacks capacity—like a child or a person in a coma. Actually there may be several other levels of our false lives that may need to be torn down before demons will leave. But surely there must be repentance and forgiveness. Repentance may take the form of, I don't want this anymore, I am not sure how it got there, but I want this thing to leave and I renounce it. Repentance may be like the Gadarene demoniac who just fell at Jesus' feet and worshipped Him. Repentance may be, Lord forgive me for my bitterness and anger, Lord forgive me for committing sexual sin (a huge open door), Lord forgive me for wanting to hurt myself, and I renounce these thoughts and activities as well. Lord forgive me for thinking occult power is where it's at. Lord, forgive me for opening the door to unclean spirits by drugs, pornography. Forgive me for this abortion. Can demons be expelled without explicit repentance? Yes, at times in an atmosphere of the Holy Spirit. But in the context of a methodical approach, I would recommend repentance and forgiveness be part of the process.

By the way, the fallout from an abortion is life altering and deep. The person(s) involved may find out many things are "aborted," "stopped short" in their lives and emotions, not to mention the guilt, shame, and deep sadness. I suggest the person(s) involved in an abortion, forgive and repent as applicable, cast out spirits of death and abortion, grief, depression and oppression, among others, and break every covenant with death.

Forgiveness may be, I forgive the person who hurt me, I forgive the person who abused me sexually as a child. Do it all in Jesus' name. Then, I repent for the sins of the generations before me in the area of [whatever], I renounce the sin, and I break generational curses in this area on both sides of my family and judgments that have come upon me. Go into generational patterns whether you are repenting or forgiving. It is possible the Holy Spirit will remind you of a similar violation in the family line or a pattern of sin in the family line. Perhaps break soul ties between yourself and the person who violated you. "I break soul ties, and all evil power, possession and control between myself and XXX in the name of Jesus and any and all imprints or parts of their soul to leave me." This is great— God is breaking the chains. More on this later. In this way *the legal grounds* for the demon to oppress is removed. This is how the devil is stopped from bringing accusation, and gets shut out of the corridors of your soul. When all the rooms in the heart belong to Jesus, there will be peace. When the demon is cleared away, a person can respond to God more easily. The blood prevails. The devil is condemned and we are declared not guilty. Romans 8:1-2: "[1] There is therefore now no condemnation to them which are in Christ Jesus, who walk not after the flesh, but after the Spirit. [2] For the law of the Spirit of life in Christ Jesus hath made me free from the law of sin and death." And that's what it's about folks, freedom from the law of sin and death and all its consequences on every level.

I don't try to cast spirits out of non-believers (as opposed to binding them if necessary) for four main reasons which overlap (1) you are in for a fight; (2) the non-believer does not have the awareness of sin; (3) there is nothing to fill the void if the spirit leaves; and (4) a non-believer is probably not aware of the demonic problem and just considers it part of his or her personality, or even welcomes it. I also don't try to cast spirits out of believers who don't see they have a problem or don't cooperate to be set free. To me, in the vast majority of deliverances, it is important to get the believer's permission, cooperation and, even better, understanding. This cannot always be the case, and I will not presume to put God in a box, but I am writing this book on the basis of reaching believers in Jesus Christ under the new covenant who want to be free. Proverbs 4:5

says to get wisdom, get understanding. But, Paul cast the spirit of divination out of a girl who was making money for her masters operating through that spirit. Even though the spirit operating in her was making a correct statement, "These men are the servants of the Most High God, which shew unto us the way of salvation," Acts 16:17, Paul discerned she was not speaking from the Spirit of God. That just shows you that people can say things that are technically true, but by the wrong spirit, and thereby not promoting the kingdom of God in holiness and truth. People can operate in the flesh (their mental/emotional/physical reasoning and desires), people can operate by unclean spirits, and people can operate through the Holy Spirit. Here is where discerning of spirits enters. Paul's spirit was grieved, so he cast the demon out. I don't know if the girl was saved later. But an earthquake in the spirit and the natural followed.

The Holy Spirit can do anything and lead us to minister in situations that do not fit any particular paradigm. However, to me, it is important that believers want to be set free and are open to the cleansing and delivering process. A woman recently came into our church. We could tell there was a problem immediately. When I questioned her, she said she had an addiction and had lost custody of her children because of it. I asked her if she wanted to be free. All of the sudden, something started operating in her, almost getting belligerent and threatening. This "person" was different from the person that was crying and presenting her problem a little earlier. She said no, she wasn't ready and left abruptly.

You say, there are physical illnesses and mental illnesses as well. That is true. But remember Jesus is the <u>Healer</u> and Deliverer. And all of this works together. A lot of physical and mental illness can be relieved, in my view, by the "un-packaging" described in this book overall. The physician in the natural has natural medicine and remedies, and the Physician in the spirit has His supernatural medicine and remedies. Again, like two different kinds of computers, there are different operating systems. Jesus got His knowledge and power from His Father and the Holy Spirit. It was not earthly wisdom or power.

Often as we pray for people, it is only natural to cast out a spirit inhabiting that place of sin or pain. As Jesus importantly taught us—a demon can leave the "house" and if there is nothing to fill that "house", he will bring seven worse than himself—again, and deliverance will be much harder the next time around. There is no spiritual neutrality. To fill the "house" we need the word of God, the presence of the Holy Spirit, the cleansing of the blood of Jesus, and hopefully some understanding of how that demon got there in the first place. "Open house" is over when there is repentance (and renunciation), and forgiveness, breaking ungodly soul ties, breaking generational patterns and curses, healing of one's emotions and so on. There is no lodging any more—the squatters are expelled and have no legal grounds to come back! Then the Holy Spirit enters and there is an abundance of peace. Squatters will come back unless you lock the doors, that is, resisting the behavior, attitudes and sins, that invited the demon in the first place, the house is occupied by the Holy Spirit and the truth of God, and you actively use your weapons, such as the word of God. Furthermore, James 4: "[7] Submit yourselves therefore to God. Resist the devil, and he will flee from you." Plead the blood of Jesus over all that concerns you. If the house is empty and unprotected, demons know how to get back in again.

A couple in my church had a squatter in a house they rented from a family member and wanted to occupy. While they had rights to the property, it took a long court battle to get the squatter out. When the squatter was leaving, he was adjusting the windows of the house to make it possible for another squatter to come in. Folks, place the blood of Jesus over the doorposts of your heart. "No Admittance—to any demon." Take authority over demons in the name of Jesus. Don't just expect the pastor to do it for you, you have authority. I only see you a short time during the week. I am happy to pray for you, but I am not with you 24 hours a day. However, the Lord is.

Demons can also enter or oppress a person because of generational curses, curses from others, such as witchcraft curses, addiction, hurt or trauma, occult practices, out of body experiences, engaging in spiritual systems not of God, an ignorant unknowing choice, and the like—something must open the door. A person has to open a door with fear, to have a spirit of fear. A person has to open a door to unbelief, to have a spirit of unbelief. A person has to open the door of anger to have a spirit of anger, violence, or rage. A person has to open a door to lust, to have a spirit of lust. And so on. When I say open a door, there may not be a knowing, "hey, come on in and get me," but perhaps a door opens through ignorance or a flash decision, exposure to drugs or the occult—both huge demonic highways, ungodly music or videos, sexual acts or porn, an ungodly attitude however unknowing, or an unwanted trauma, encounter, anger or abuse. Please note, however, there are people deliberately operating in the occult who are literally asking demons to enter them and give them knowledge and power. As we walk deeper and deeper into the waters of the Jordan, more and more will come off and there are levels in which demons will be cast out. Consider an accident or violation that causes trauma. Spirits of fear can enter the person so traumatized. Spirits can pass generationally—familiar spirits, perversion, depression, suicide, occult related spirits, sicknesses, infirmities and others. Some ministers also have dealt with spirits passed through blood transfusions, such as the trauma, fear, or anger attached to the donor's blood. Have at it! Command the spirits to leave. With regard to familiar spirits, believers must be willing to let go of familiar spirits and permit their identity in Christ to grow. Familiar spirits not only know about us, and transmit information about us to other receptive demons, but pass on generational dispositions, thoughts or feelings. Familiar spirits are thought to be used by mediums to contact the dead. But there really is no such thing as contacting the dead; the spirits are only contacting other impersonating demons and transmitting information. Familiar spirits are used in divination, i.e. telling the future through hidden knowledge.

Also, sins involving the occult such as out of body experiences, meditation, witchcraft, palm reading, astrology, magic, going to a psychic or medium, mind control systems, Santeria, voodoo, or any other occult practices, just to name a few, are intrinsically demonic, and open the door of demonic oppression and curses for the participant and generations to come. Add to that pornography, ungodly music with messages that are not of God, traumas, physical, sexual, emotional and mental abuse, use of drugs and alcohol, sexual relations which transfer spirits, and other entry ways. Just about any push from the enemy can be an open door. We live in a spiritual universe, whether we understand it, like it, believe it, or not. We are spiritual beings, and we are very vulnerable to spiritual influence unless we have discernment and understand spiritual warfare. Again, consider these verses from Ephesians 2: "[1] And you hath he quickened, who were dead in trespasses and sins—ok, we started out spiritually dead, but Christ made us alive; [2] Wherein in time past ye walked according to the course of this world—we walked in conformity with the world, but there was a lot of influence, see the next phrase, according to the <u>prince of the power of the air, the spirit that now worketh in the children of disobedience</u>: [3] Among whom also we all had our conversation in times past in the lusts of our flesh, fulfilling the desires of the flesh and of the mind; and were by nature the children of wrath, even as others." This is what happens when we are under the influence of evil spirits.

The prince of the power of the air, Satan himself, is bending and distorting and suppressing all of reality and the truth of God, and <u>working in the children of disobedience</u>, who are walking after the course of this world, whatever that is at any particular time. Many people are ignorant of the workings of the kingdom of God and the kingdom of Satan and are a target for the enemy. The enemy displays his dazzling chaos in front of people's eyes, and they become transfixed and drawn in by it, but the end is destruction. Furthermore, the prince of the power of the air works in the children of disobedience to manifest his plans on earth, and work in their lives personally. There is a threefold cord, then, the prince of the power of the air, the course of this world, and the flesh. Satan's hierarchy has influence over individual lives, homes, neighborhoods, cities, territories and nations, and over different realms of influence in the world, such as politics, religion, finance, education, or entertainment. Demonic entities can also enter in to the soul and physical realm and oppress a person's soul (mind, will and emotions) and body. People who are not saved, are spiritually dead and are vulnerable. I believe our spirits come alive and belong to the Lord when we are saved, for we can now connect with the Father through the blood of Jesus and are born again by the Spirit. But the rest is open game which has not been delivered, sanctified and under the control of the Spirit of God. The prince of the power of the air is constantly jamming the air-waves with ungodly garbage and lies, blasphemies and distortions, and controlling nations, cities, localities, families, institutions and sometimes churches. The first words the devil spoke on earth were lies, and he has not changed since. Test the spirits, John writes, not every spirit is of God. I John 4:1-2. When we gain dominion over our own lives through Jesus Christ, then homes, territories, cities, nations can change.

Often when believers start their walk with the Lord they may be set free from a certain spirit of addiction or lust, but then as they walked further, there were spirits of sorrow and fear or familiar spirits. Sometimes there are spirits of infirmity or types of sicknesses. In each level of cleansing, there are spirits that must leave. There are habitations of these demons in our souls, based on attitudes, traumas, rejection, false adaptations and the like that should be collapsed, so that the demonic trespasser no longer has a house in which to dwell. Be led of the Holy Spirit as to what to address. Furthermore, each believer must deal with emotions that separate the individual from God, others and themselves, for the demonic house of control to further collapse. Jesus said that "My house shall be called a house of prayer, but you have made it a den of thieves." Matthew 21:13. Aren't we the temple of the Holy Spirit, and responsible to clear that temple of the thieves? Demons, (one type of thieves because they devour our true lives), are only cast out by commanding them to leave in the name of Jesus. You cannot starve a demon. You cannot counsel a demon, you cannot love a demon out, you cannot convince it to leave by being nice, you cannot buy it off—it will fool you, bite you in the behind, and remain in its territory—you! It must be cast out. I believe that if the sins are dealt with, generational patterns and curses are addressed, and the emotional elements behind the sins experience a measure of healing, then the demons should be expelled easily. It is easier for it to leave with repentance, forgiveness, breaking generational curses and so on. After that, minister healing. This, again, reduces the fuel for sin. Choice becomes liberated. When lies are replaced with truth, and healing begins, then demons must leave.

Jesus talked about the strong man, who was the controller of the house. Matthew 12: "²⁸ But if I cast out devils by the Spirit of God, then the kingdom of God is come unto you. ²⁹Or else how can one enter into a strongman's house, and spoil his goods, except he first bind the strongman? and then he will spoil his house." We know the story about the strongman, but how does the strongman really enter? A person invites strong man into their house perhaps to protect them, or the strongman tricks his way in, but now the strongman is controlling the house (you) and you are serving that strong man, or running around in the back of the house not knowing what to do--the real person is in hiding. The strong man can also be a false persona or alternate personality that has come through adaptation to external influences or trauma, for example, but then it runs the house. Where is the real person? Your enemy is the strongman which may be a demon or false self you embraced to protect and defend yourself, which you thought was smart at first, but then you forgot who you were, or the real you never matured. It can be a familiar spirit which runs the house. Maybe that strongman is some spirit you have taken on through occult practices for protection, knowledge, or power. Who and what is the ruler of your house? All these were brought into the house to give strength, reduce anxiety and internal conflicts, bring protection or attract love, but then they started to rule the house. The real inhabitant (the true person in the image of God) is like a tiny weak person under the bed, or perhaps a shadow in a cage. We need to repent for such compromises (and all compromises).

Perhaps the strong man is a spirit passed on through the generations. It can be the overlord controlling all the other unclean spirits. Another view: You may be the strong man, you may be the controller, you may have a false identity or an identity you created as a young child to protect yourself, tough guy, manipulator, shy person, someone of the opposite sex or fluidly taking an identity that controls your house, until Someone stronger comes, when we can give control to that stronger, awesomely loving, Lord Jesus Christ. That requires us to trust God, rather than trusting ourselves, and trust can only be re-established by the layer by layer healing of our hearts, and the layer by layer foundation of truth and holiness from the word of God. Our lives will always be controlled by something or someone unless we trust God. It comes down to establishing trust again in broken hearts, so our hearts may be united to fear His name and praise His name. Again, Psalms 86:11–12: "[11] Teach me thy way, O LORD; I will walk in thy truth: unite my heart to fear thy name. [12] I will praise thee, O Lord my God, with all my heart: and I will glorify thy name for evermore." As we repair the breaches, the demonic invaders must leave.

Just a little side note here: Accursed objects can bring a curse and demons to your house, such as occult books, ungodly books and music, idols and art from other religions, ankhs, idols, horoscopes, tarot cards, Ouija boards, occult jewelry and clothes, some trinket or mask you got on your trip overseas, drugs, and sin-related objects. Deuteronomy 7:25-26. Demons are attached to them. "You must burn their idols in fire, and do not desire the silver or gold with which they are made. Do not take it or it will become a snare to you, for it is detestable to the LORD your God. [26] Do not bring any detestable objects into your home, for then you will be set apart for destruction just like them. You must utterly detest such things, for they are set apart for destruction." Destroy what is ungodly, get rid of what is detestable, and sanctify items that are spiritually neutral for ordinary use, unless the Lord tells you to get rid of such objects. I promise you, that by getting ungodly items out of your house, a new peace will enter. It is an important point that everything we have, must be capable of being part of God's kingdom and plan for our lives.

Also, most of us are aware that persons using occult power will seek an object, picture, clipping of hair, jewelry or clothing from the person to be cursed or controlled. This enables the transference of spirits through a curse. This isn't exactly about ungodly soul ties, but these items can be points of contact for transference of spirits. And what about those tattoos—pentagrams, skulls, gang identification—seriously, what are you attracting in the spirit world? I once saw a woman wearing an ankh, pentagram, and peace symbol (upside down broken cross) around her neck. Her face looked like it had a mask, you couldn't even discern the real person.

Appendix B has a description of spirits described in the Bible and simple commands to cast them out. Their time has ended. Remember how the demons cried to Jesus when being expelled, "Are You are trying to torment us before the time?" Matthew 8:29. No, the time of torment has not come yet, but the time to leave the believer who is in submission to the Lord Jesus *has come*. You as a believer have authority over demons, and you are encouraged to act on that authority and not be ignorant, and you are going to feel better. The list in Appendix B is not all inclusive. Some people in the ministry of deliverance get into specific personal names of demons and principalities. That's fine if such an approach is revealed to you; but I do know that we can address demons by function—spirit of addiction, sadness, control, for example. If you look at the Gadarene demoniac in Mark 5 you will notice there were many spirits operating in him before Jesus set him free—sadness, self-destruction, lewdness, separation, rebellion, supernatural strength, and more, but they were all under the strong man, Legion. Legion represents about six thousand spirits. Jesus just went for Legion. Mark 5:9: "And he asked him, What is thy name? And he answered, saying, My name is Legion: for we are many." [10] And he besought him much that he would not send them (plural) away out of the country. [11] Now there was there nigh unto the mountains a great herd of swine feeding. [12] And all the devils besought him, saying, Send us into the swine, that we may enter into them. [13] And forthwith Jesus gave them leave. Remember that they all did not have the same function, and He didn't call them out by name individually, but they all left. Also they wanted to inhabit something, and the swine were available. Demons desire to inhabit, people, animals, places and objects—probably in that order.

When ministering deliverance to a person, always follow the trail of where and how the spirit entered. Repent, renounce, break soul ties if necessary, generational patterns and curses, allow the Lord to enter traumas for healing. Let the Holy Spirit be your guide. Remember God's ultimate plan: Psalms 23: "[3] He restoreth my soul:

He leads me in the paths of righteousness for His name's sake." And He gives us the power to bring His plan to pass. Luke 10:19 "Behold, I give unto you power to tread on serpents and scorpions, and over all the power of the enemy: and nothing shall by any means hurt you."

Jesus said the Holy Spirit is like a wind, and it blows where it wants and you can hear the sound of it, but don't know where it comes from or where it goes John 3:8. Likewise, the principalities and powers that run a city or nation, and demons that run a home or a person, are like a tornado or hurricane. You can see the path of destruction. Hurricanes or tornados bring a path of death. Some of these hurricanes and tornados in our society have been the lies the enemy has spoken on sexual freedom, some are lies about who we are and identities, some are lies about money and love. Now we have 3000 abortions a day in the United States. Some of these hurricanes have destroyed the family, have mocked and marginalized the things of God. Hurricanes blow through families when one member is caught up in drugs or criminal activities. There are tornados of sickness and financial loss. So I prefer the wind of the Holy Spirit that releases the life of God, to the tornados, hurricanes and lies of the devil. Jesus is the Way the Truth and the Life, and the Lord told His people, choose life.

THIRD LEVEL: CURSES

The next level of cleansing is the curse level, and this cuts across many types of curses.

1. Generational curses and patterns of sins.

Exodus 20:5 "Thou shalt not bow down thyself to them, nor serve them: for I the LORD thy God am a jealous God, visiting the iniquity of the fathers upon the children unto the third and fourth generation of them that hate me; ⁶ And shewing mercy unto thousands of them that love me, and keep my commandments." (The second half is the good part.)

While the new birth gives us a start—remember infancy is a "start," pressing into the power of the cross allows believers to be (1) healed and delivered; (2) reduce the fuel for sin; (3) liberate the power to choose again; (4) become what God wants us to be and do in this world; and (5) release us into the inheritance and destiny God has for us. If you want the highest, we must allow the Lord to deal with us on the generational level, as well as all the other levels for healing and deliverance. The resurrection empowers us and establishes our new nature in a new divine life and destiny. Upgrade requires new appropriation of "up-grace."

Bottom line it is much easier to follow Jesus when one is not in emotional pain—He bore our griefs and sorrows, (Isaiah 53:4); or trying to maneuver life with a broken heart—He came to heal the brokenhearted, (Luke 4:18); when we are not living out lies—the truth makes us free, (John 8:32); living under generational curses, and judgments—we will get to that in a bit (Exodus 20:5, Galatians 3:13); or demonically oppressed (Luke 4:18). Again, inner healing and deliverance reduce the fuel for sin, and lives out of God's order and blessing. (We _do_ have to agree with the word of God). Deliverance also opens the door for God to fill us in a greater capacity and experience life in a greater capacity. It is true that we all have problems of our own making, but even many of these have grabbed ahold of us because of generational patterns and curses. We carry on what has gone before us, whether we realize it or not—so much has been set in motion spiritually before we even arrived on the scene. God wants us to grow, be blessed, increase, be fruitful, fellowship with Him, help others, expand, have joy and touch the world. Frankly, I don't want to live with the baggage of previous generations. They suffered enough. In Hebrews 12:1 the Lord tell us to lay down the weights (and sins) that easily beset us. What could "beset" us more than the weights and sins from previous generations of our families? This is a way to let them go.

What is a generational curse, and what is a generational blessing? Certainly it has to do with failure and blessing, sin and righteousness, gain and loss. A generational curse becomes the vehicle to act out brokenness and sinfulness. Mark Virkler, in his book Prayers that Heal the Heart, talks about "sin energy," and sin dwells in us—it is something that fuels the disasters in our lives. Paul the apostle, writes, I do what I don't want to do and what I want to do, I can't. Romans 7:17. In my book, Restoration NOW!, I emphasize the effects of a generational curse. A generational curse in an area leads to a predisposition, bent or vulnerability to repeat a pattern of behavior, way of thinking/feeling, or type of failure or loss from a previous generation. With regard to sin it is the non-choice choice in the sense that our hearts are steered easily in this direction. The curse is the spiritual channel whereby people act out brokenness and desires in a particular sinful pattern because that spiritual door was opened by a previous generation. Following that pattern is not inevitable, but there is a vulnerability. There are also patterns of sickness or types of destruction, such as early death, or failure in education or business, that are generational. You didn't do anything, but generations have failed in some area or experienced loss. A generational blessing, on the other hand, may be a generational disposition to succeed in a certain area, a calling, ability, or easier access to a divine destiny.

Additionally, there may be demonic influences that reinforce this. A generational curse or pattern of sin may target us in certain areas, where another person might be totally free. So, there can be a predisposition (automatic built-in desire) for a type of sin because of generational curses. "(F)or I the Lord thy God am a jealous God, visiting the iniquity [sins and moral illness] of the fathers upon the children unto the third and fourth generation of them that hate me." Exodus 20:5.

Our solution: Galatians 3:13 - 14 (NKJV) "[13] Christ has redeemed us from the curse of the law, having become a curse for us (for it is written, *"Cursed is everyone who hangs on a tree"*), [14] that the blessing of Abraham might come upon the Gentiles in Christ Jesus, that we might receive the promise of the Spirit through faith." Jesus broke every curse on the cross. He took it, He became it, so that the blessings of Abraham might come to us, and that we might receive the promise of the Spirit through faith.

A lot of people think that we don't need to do anything about generational curses, because Jesus became a curse for us. Therefore, we don't have to deal with it—just sit back and relax. Well, Jesus became sin for us too, but we still have to repent. Jesus took our sicknesses and diseases, but He also equipped the body of Christ with faith and the gifts of the Holy Spirit, to pray for healing. Jesus gave us eternal life, but we have to want it and ask for it. Jesus paid it all, but we must "appropriate" or "take Him up on" what He did for us at the cross. Likewise, the Holy Spirit shows us the patterns of generational curses, and other types of curses.

The Lord states at the beginning of the Ten Commandments that sin can be passed on from generation to generation. By the way, blessings can be passed on also. What are some examples of sins and patterns of behavior passed on from generation to generation that we see all the time? Here is a short list: Alcoholism and other addictions, abuse, sexual sin—that is any and all sexual expression of whatever variety outside of the Biblical definition of marriage, control, religious spirits, pride, occult power and activity, bitterness, fear, family breakdown, suicide, poverty, and violence. Whether we like it or not, sin opens the doors for other generations down the line to be damaged and actually defiled with the same problems—it is the law of the seed. There may be demons that pass from generation to generation. Remember we are spiritual beings, and subject to spiritual forces. For example, there can be generational curses of poverty, not just lack of money, but inability to look forward to a future and get ahead from whatever cause. We must backtrack how this happened. It may be through ignorance of the word of God or lack of faith in the the Lord that may have come through brokenness in a certain area which creates an attitude of hopelessness, passivity, or compromise. God is no respecter of persons; He will help us move forward in life wherever we started. There may be generations that earned money illegally or did not tithe, or failed to give to the poor or stole from people, engaged in criminal behavior, or did not care about or understand the importance of education or acquiring a skill. There can be abusive behavior and disobedience that keeps people from coming to their potential and growing, limitations due to environment or family, generational discrimination. Let's backtrack. The Lord wants us to know that poverty can be overcome, He preached the gospel to the poor, but the poor have to receive it, because God wants to release the blessings of Abraham to His children. People's ability to have faith in an area becomes subdued and battered due to generational curses. The good news is that there is a way out. Don't forget, Jesus came out of a tomb.

As I wrote, there are blessings that pass through generations, and there are curses. Let me just summarize by saying, there is power in the blood, the "blood" being in a general sense your DNA/bloodline, passed on by your parents and ancestry. I am using a shortcut term, the "blood." It includes among other things, who we are, what we look like, callings and blessings, demons and curses, gifts and abilities, failures, control, self-reliance, dependency, freedom, illness, mental and physical, and health. It is possible that many doors opened up for you and you were given favor as a "payment" for the obedience and righteousness of previous generations, or conversely, you experienced loss because of their disobedience. Only the blood of Jesus Christ interrupts the power of our family bloodline or sanctifies that which is good; which is another important point, but not necessarily the focus of this book. We have all been given generational blessings and gifts, but are these going to be sanctified and put under the direction of the Holy Spirit and the purposes of God, or used to serve our own little gods?

I believe, a person starts reducing the fuel for sin and fuel for failure and limited destinies by breaking generational curses and patterns of sin. In a total package that means taking down the strong-man, repentance, breaking generational curses and patterns, deliverance from demonic oppression, healing of hurts and traumas. I believe generational pain and trauma is passed on as well. We carry the sorrows of previous generations. Moving on from there, take another step as Apostle Robert Henderson has described in his *Courts of Heaven* books (which I recommend) and break the judgments against us for these personal and generational sins, so that our true destinies, callings, blessings, healings, answers to prayer, etc., can be released. What is holding back the true life? What is holding back the blessings and answers to prayers? We can go to the courts of heaven and plead on the basis of the blood of Jesus to be released from the judgments and penalties against us due to our own sin or in our family lines, entering in with repentance.

Your physical and spiritual bloodline affects not only how you look, and perhaps whether you are good in music, or mathematic skills, or carry certain sicknesses or diseases, but also the patterns of behavior and our very purpose in life. The only blood and bloodline that is stronger than our own is the blood of Jesus which cleanses us. We need the new birth, and new spiritual DNA to erase and interrupt the destruction of many generations, so that the foundation of many generations can be built up and the breaches repairs. Isaiah 58:12. The blood of Jesus has power. That doesn't mean that suddenly we get a new blood type through transfusion, it means that the blood of Jesus sanctifies our spiritual "bloodline" and interrupts our spiritual DNA (physical, moral, spiritual and emotional bent) consistent with the word and will of God, and gives us power over the power of sin and the works of the devil. He interrupts our patterns of limitation and destruction by His cleansing blood, and by adoption into the family of God—a new ancestry. We have a new and higher destiny, a God dimension of life. He changes us from sinners and children of the devil, to saints and children of God.

There are three phases of revival. One dealing with the past, one with the present, and one with the future. The past goes to the inaugural sermon of Jesus, Luke 4: "[18] The Spirit of the Lord is upon me, because he hath anointed me to preach the gospel to the poor; he hath sent me to heal the brokenhearted, to preach deliverance to the captives, and recovering of sight to the blind, to set at liberty them that are bruised, [19] To preach the acceptable year of the Lord." There is a reason why the day of God's favor, meaning the "acceptable year of the Lord" is placed at the end of the verse. Notice the progression. When we go through the phases of healing and deliverance, we can stand in righteousness, and finally, enter into our purpose, and the obedient, submitted and blessed life based on what God has done for us and what the Lord has ordained for us. In short, it is the day of God's favor. We enter into the blessings of knowing and following Him. We follow the pattern and journey God has for us, not our own. This allows us to fully engage in the present as the person God created us to be, and fulfill a future designed by God.

Where is the foundation? It is in the blood. The blood of Jesus cleanses and restores and rebuilds our true identity, and replaces our humanity founded in sin (and the tree of the knowledge of good and evil) to one rooted and grounded in God's love (through the tree of life, the cross). It took the cross of Jesus Christ; it was no easy process. It cost the death of God the Son. Through the Word of God, the name of Jesus, the blood of Jesus, the power of the Holy Spirit, the predispositions and vulnerabilities of our own bloodlines can be changed, to enable us to make new, divine choices and walk in a new divine identity and destiny.

John 1:12 - 13 (NLT) "[12] But to all who believed him and accepted him, he gave the right to become children of God. [13]They are reborn! This is not a physical birth resulting from human passion or plan—this rebirth comes from God."

When Jesus came to earth, John prophesied "And now also the axe is laid unto the root of the trees: therefore, every tree which brings not forth good fruit is hewn down, and cast into the fire." Matthew 3:10. What kind of trees was he talking about? He was talking about trees of unrighteousness, rebellion, unbelief, idolatry, deception, sorrow, grief, mental illness, addiction, pain, bitterness, sexual sin, occult involvement, and more, in our own lives and passed through family lines. God wants nothing less *than death and life*, a radical transformation, destroying the roots of the trees planted by the enemy through the generations, and then planting trees of righteousness with the word of God. Our pattern is nothing less than the cross and resurrection. So the old generational trees of unrighteousness must be unrooted and the new godly seeds of truth planted so we can be rooted and grounded in love. LET THOSE SEEDS GROW AND SEE WHAT A CROP GOD CAN BUILD.

Further, the growth of the new trees is going to depend on whether the soil of our hearts is receptive. When you read the parable of the sower and the seed, the main thing is the soil, not the seed. The seed is unchangeable but the soil is going to determine the success of the seed. Our lives cannot bear fruit if the soil is shallow, toxic, hard, or overrun with weeds and thorns. People can receive the same seed of the word, but the growth of the seed and whether it fulfills its purpose depends on the soil. Hosea 10:12 says, "Sow to yourselves in righteousness, reap in mercy; break up your fallow (unplowed) ground: for *it is* time to seek the LORD, till he come and rain righteousness upon you." The hard ground of our hearts needs to be softened with the rain of the Holy Spirit, repentance, intimate experiences of God's love, rejection of mindsets against the will of God, healing of brokenness, and other experiences with the Lord. This hardness of heart can be generational as well.

Here are some verses on generational sins and curses if you don't believe me:

We see in Exodus 20:5 that the sins and iniquities of the fathers are visited on the children to the third and fourth generations.

Exodus 34:6-7 (NLT) "[6] He passed in front of Moses and said, "I am the LORD, I am the LORD, the merciful and gracious God. I am slow to anger and rich in unfailing love and faithfulness. [7] I show this unfailing love to many thousands by forgiving every kind of sin and rebellion. Even so I do not leave sin unpunished, but I punish the children for the sins of their parents to the third and fourth generations."

Numbers 14: "[18] The LORD *is* longsuffering, and of great mercy, forgiving iniquity and transgression, and by no means clearing *the guilty*, visiting the iniquity of the fathers upon the children unto the third and fourth *generation*."

Leviticus 26: "[39] And they that are left of you shall pine away in their iniquity in your enemies' lands; and also in the iniquities of their fathers shall they pine away with them."

Jeremiah 32:18 (TMSG) "[18] You're loyal in your steadfast love to thousands upon thousands—but you also make children live with the fallout from their parents' sins. Great and powerful God, named GOD-of-the-Angel-Armies," ... .

Hosea 4:6 (TMSG) "[6] My people are ruined because they don't know what's right or true. Because you've turned your back on knowledge, I've turned my back on you priests. Because you refuse to recognize the revelation of God, I'm no longer recognizing your children. Hosea 4:6 (NKJV) [6] My people are destroyed for lack of knowledge. Because you have rejected knowledge, I also will reject you from being priest for Me; Because you have forgotten the law of your God, I also will forget your children."

Nehemiah 1:5-9: "[5] And said, I beseech thee, O LORD God of heaven, the great and terrible God, that keepeth covenant and mercy for them that love him and observe his commandments: [6] Let thine ear now be attentive, and thine eyes open, that thou mayest hear the prayer of thy servant, which I pray before thee now, day and night, for the children of Israel thy servants, and confess the sins of the children of Israel, which we have sinned against thee: both I and my father's house have sinned. [7] We have dealt very corruptly against thee, and have not kept the commandments, nor the statutes, nor the judgments, which thou commandest thy servant Moses. [8] Remember, I beseech thee, the word that thou commandest thy servant Moses, saying, *If* ye transgress, I will scatter you abroad among the nations: [9] But *if* ye turn unto me, and keep my commandments, and do them; though there were of you cast out unto the uttermost part of the heaven, *yet* will I gather them from thence, and will bring them unto the place that I have chosen to set my name there."

Daniel 9: "⁵We have sinned, and have committed iniquity, and have done wickedly, and have rebelled, even by departing from thy precepts and from thy judgments: ⁶Neither have we hearkened unto thy servants the prophets, which spake in thy name to our kings, our princes, and our fathers, and to all the people of the land."

Then in verse 16 of chapter 9, Daniel prays, "O Lord, according to all thy righteousness, I beseech thee, let thine anger and thy fury be turned away from thy city Jerusalem, thy holy mountain: because for our sins, and for the iniquities of our fathers, Jerusalem and thy people are become a reproach to all that are about us." If you read this chapter you will see that Daniel confessed his sins, the sins of his fathers, and the sins of the nation, to lift the judgments they were experiencing as a people. The desolations were not a surprise. The people of God under the Mosaic covenant were told precisely what would happen based on the law and as declared by the prophets (who God sent in His mercy) if they disobeyed the Lord, but they did it anyway. Daniel, likewise relying on the covenant of God and His mercies, made supplications that the judgments be lifted. He realized the time of captivity was over. Huge demonic forces were holding back Judah's deliverance from Babylon, but through his collective, generational and personal repentance, the legal grounds for their opposition to Judah's release were defeated. It is interesting that someone had to intercede to bring in the prophetic promise to pass. We may have been promised many things in the word of God and even by personal prophecy. However, there are times we must repent for ourselves, and repent for our fathers, for the patterns of iniquity and the curses to be broken, and ask the Lord that the judgments that have held back the favor and blessings and destiny of God be released against us through the blood of Jesus, which has paid these judgments in full.

Matthew 6:12 (NKJV) "¹²And forgive us our debts, as we forgive our debtors." Notice there is the concept of collective debt. Because sins and debts accumulate over generations.

The Bible is clearly a family history. Adam the rebellious first son of Father God, had a rebellious first son, who had a rebellious first son. God puts our rebellion and sin before our eyes to show us a lesson that each seed reproduces after its own kind, and if you sow spiritual seeds of death, you will reap them for generations. Sin may be enjoyable, living by our own rules and thoughts may feed body and soul, but will you like it all so much when it destroys your children, lifts the hand of God's protection, blocks God's blessings or causes generational misery? Spiritual life or death travels by bloodlines. God, Who set up this pattern of families in the beginning, understood that in order for the race of Adam to come back to spiritual life, its lineage needed to be traced to a new Adam (Jesus) wherein a new spiritual bloodline could be established. God provided for the death of the old Adamic line at the cross so a new line in Jesus (the Second Adam) could be established. Everything ends and begins at the cross.

This new bloodline would be initiated by our new Father, God, Who plants the seed of life in us through our open hearts receiving the Word (Jesus). The new seed of the word is given life by the Holy Spirit, Who nurtures the seed, just as He overshadowed Mary who conceived the Messiah, by the Seed of God Himself. This is in contrast to the ungodly seed of our old spiritual father Satan who planted lies in us, to reproduce the false god of self, leading to death, and replicating his own wicked, vacant, depraved self. For those of us who believe in Jesus, the result is that we are in Him and He is in us. We are the body of Christ on earth and we grow into the stature of Christ, and our destination is heaven instead of hell.

Is there a way to a blessed bloodline? Of course. God never leaves us without remedy—God had a remedy before there was a problem. Jesus is the Lamb Slain from the Foundation of the World. The cross of Jesus Christ puts to death our old natures, and gives us the new nature of Jesus Christ. He takes our condemnation, and the curses that have been laid upon us since Adam. Now, I believe that every family has certain dispositions, open doors, areas of vulnerability, and I believe that we must deal with those dispositions, open doors and vulnerabilities—what is attractive to me, what draws me in or causes me to fall, may be totally uninteresting to you. A person can be targeted in a certain area and another person experiences complete protection or couldn't care less. Some people fall into certain sins easily and for others it would take an effort to cross the barrier into that sin. As I have said before, some people are attracted to the occult. I have never had an interest in the occult. I tried hard to meditate when I was in college and it lasted about 20 minutes. I went out once a man who was into the occult, a very nice looking man, but I was not interested in him at all. On the other hand, someone else may be totally drawn to such a person, and find it exciting to speak a demonic chant inside a pentagram.

Frankly, I believe that the issue of generational patterns and curses (with regard to the sin issue) moves in part in this way: When we experience emotional hurt or damage, even emotional damage due to our own sin, or we are sinned against, or the opportunity presents itself, the generational curse predisposes us to a particular sinful pattern to act out our brokenness.

We all get things from our families; histories and inherited temperament—some good, some bad, some generational, some imprinted into our very cells. However, engaging in acts and attitudes outside the will of God requires a choice, no matter how predisposed an individual is— just like any number of other behaviors. Despite the ease with which a person falls into any sin or pattern of living (I call these "non-choice choices"), that predisposition still reflects a heart the Lord wants to forgive, heal and restore. A generational curse can also be a pattern of hurt, loss, sickness or pain in a family. For example, all the men in the family line die early. The good news is that we can recognize these patterns by the power of the Holy Spirit, and break them.

It is true that if we do something different we can have a different, result, but it is hard to <u>do something different without being someone different</u>.

What triggers the curse when we are dealing with sinful activities or mindsets? Here is another view—needs early in life that are left unmet, traumas, abuse, feelings of abandonment, environmental opportunities and pressure, loss, rejection, inadequacy, and so forth. The generation before you can't give you what they don't have. They were living out their own issues. In order to resolve these losses, we reach to our own solutions, and these solutions are the set up from the generations before us. Somebody opened the door.

When we come to Jesus, He shows us the ways to resolve our emptiness, losses, relational needs in a godly way, by the power of the word, and the Holy Spirit. Because of the new birth through the shed blood of Jesus and the Holy Spirit our choices can be sanctified once again.

INIQUITY: In sum, patterns of sin pass through families. Accordingly, as God has clarified in scripture the generational reach of iniquity, He has also prescribed a generational release from iniquity. At the cross, "the Lord has laid on Him the iniquity of us all." Isaiah 53:6. He took upon Himself the iniquity of us all—notice ALL, the entire network of blame, brokenness, moral illness, perversion, guilt and sin that spans from the Garden of Eden to the gates of heaven. Thank God, it is the work of Jesus Christ to undo this specific work of the devil. Jesus came to lay the axe to the root of the trees of family line sins and curses.

How do you know you have a generational curse working in your life? You repeat the patterns in your family history, such as: (a) family breakup, addiction, suicide, or sickness in a certain area; (b) no one seems to get ahead economically or graduate from school, criminal behavior and imprisonment; (c) sexual, physical, emotional, verbal abuse, sexual sins, incest; (d) different forms of hatred the family harbors, occult involvement; (e) continued patterns of sin, brokenness and failure; (f) repeated accidents, deaths, or losses.

There can be many outward evidences of curses, but let's look at the inward ones—feeling oppressed or depressed all your life, emptiness and lack of confidence about yourself or identity, just knowing you can't make it in a certain area, unusually bad choices, inferiority, fear and shame, being a victim of abuse or perpetrator of it, sadness, rejection. These are all disasters.

BUT BECAUSE OF JESUS, Isaiah 58:12 states: "And they that

shall be of thee shall build up the old waste places; you shall raise up the foundations of many generations; and you shall be called, the repairer of the breach, the restorer of paths to dwell in." The work of God is to repair the inner person. To those individuals who will yield themselves, God will do in them a work that will raise up the foundations that have been in disrepair for many generations. If there are generational patterns in your family line, God can stop it in you. The cross intervenes. For families left as "old waste places" in brokenness, God will rise up a new life in any person who yields themselves. <u>Remember there are also generational strengths and blessings.</u>

The ministers of righteousness are sent to repair the breaches, so that our family lines no longer carry defective patterns and curses through the ravages of sin, but are clean, whole, quickened to live in the relationship with the Lord.

Families for generations have crumbled and fallen. Their foundations have been broken, for these foundations were made of lies, going back to the original lies in the Garden of Eden. When Adam and Eve's foundation on the truth of the Word of God slipped to the perverted lies expounded by an outlaw from heaven, the foundations of the human race (spiritually, morally, economically, socially, governmentally, and emotionally) became faulty ever since. On the other hand, build your life on the Rock and the foundation will be secure. Jesus came to redeem us from the curse of the law, that is the penalties, including judgments, of collective, generational disobedience that fall on individuals. To "redeem" means to "release, preserve, rescue, deliver, liberate cut loose, sever, to free, to ransom." "Christ hath redeemed us from the curse of the law being made a curse for us: for it is written, cursed is everyone that hangs on a tree." Galatians 3:13. Jesus took our judgment on the cross, by taking on Himself the <u>penalties</u> and <u>curses</u> from sin, as defined in the <u>book</u> of the <u>law</u>.

All humanity's sin and the effect thereof, generational sins, family line curses, judgments, sickness, and domination by Satan are erased and eradicated at the cross. We all are derived spiritually from the original seed of Satan, the lies that Adam and Eve swallowed, but we all can be redeemed by the new word, the Living Word, Jesus, inside of us. When sin is sown in one generation it reaps a crop in others, perhaps of a larger and more dangerous volume, because one seed sown can produce many others. There is always a harvest. But on the other hand, when righteousness enters, that can produce a harvest of life for generations. Appendix C has a sample prayer to break generational curses. The fact of the matter is, in most families hardly anyone closes the doors to generational curses, because they don't know what they are or how to end a curse, or even if they exist. So perhaps you are the person to do it, for yourself and your family, and raise up the foundations of many generations.

2. Curses from disobedience

In Deuteronomy 28 the Lord told His people that if they obeyed Him they would be blessed, and if they disobeyed Him, they would be cursed. There was a list of the blessings and a list of the curses: Column A and Column B. The concept was fairly simple. The <u>first</u> reason was and is as follows (the <u>second</u> and <u>third</u> reasons described below are equally as important): The earth is under a curse because of sin. The world and world system are under the influence of the prince of the power of the air, and evil principalities and powers. The ground is cursed, creation is under the curse, bloodlines are cursed, life outside of God's will is cursed, no matter how happy or prosperous someone's existence seems to be, and all people are sinners and slaves to sin and sin's consequences and are cursed. All people experience results and penalties from breaking God's laws, whether they know it, believe it, or not. Existence on earth follows the law of sin and death. Total relief from the curse is not going to happen until Jesus comes to rules and reign and there is a new heaven and a new earth. Also, creation is waiting for the curse to be broken through the manifestation of the sons of God. See Romans 8:19. But the Lord established a plan to provide relief from the curse to His people and affirmative blessing and favor <u>before</u> He took the curse of the law on the cross. Deuteronomy 28 is that plan—obedience was the key to the covenant of protection and favor.

The history of Deuteronomy 28 goes to the various covenants that the Lord established starting with Adam, Noah, Abraham and Moses. Most relevant for this explanation is that the Lord established a chosen people through Abraham. Because of Abraham's faith all the nations of the world would be blessed, and Abraham and his descendants would be blessed—part of the Abrahamic covenant. He later established and instructed His chosen people from Abraham's promised son Isaac through the "Mosaic covenant" of the law. The essence was, if they worshipped Him, put Him first, obeyed Him as He described in the law, they would be sheltered, and under the umbrella of His blessing—they would not be subject to the "curses" that other nations experienced, including curses from breaking God's laws. Further, He would positively bless their land, livestock, finances, their families and their nation, they would be the head and not the tail, blessed going in and going out, above and not beneath, and they would prosper and be in good health, and have number ONE standing as the people of God among the nations. In short, they would have divine favor; not just any kind of favor, but supernatural favor with God behind it.

On the other hand, if they disobeyed Him, worshipped other gods and so forth, allowed themselves to be dragged down into the idolatry, immorality, and wickedness of their neighbors, they would come out from under the umbrella of His protection and provision and affirmative favor and love, and be cursed, like the nations around them—actually more. Let me explain: Here is the second supernatural dimension to their problem; they would be more subject to harm because they had knowledge of God and rejected Him deliberately. Their heathen neighbors didn't know the difference. Consequently, the Lord would actually fight against them. They were supposed to be a witness of God's love and truth on earth; rejecting that love and truth they became witnesses of God's judgment (and subsequent mercy at times). God let them know (continually) that He would be angry and allow them to experience the curses described in Deuteronomy 28, as a lesson to themselves and their neighbors. Read Deuteronomy 28 for yourself. God's people were told that the consequences from disobeying God included everything from poverty to sickness, to being overcome by enemies, not enjoying the fruits of one's labor, children in captivity, personal captivity and more. These consequences didn't solely affect the actual "sinner" but also their family, and, if widespread enough, the entire nation. More precisely, He would be provoked by the rejection of His goodness. So it was not just that they ventured out from under the umbrella of protection and were subject to the general law of sin and death, and the demonic and generational destruction experienced by other nations. Because of their collective disobedience they provoked the Lord based on that special favor and revelation given to them. He told them to choose life—He laid the whole picture out in front of them. He listed the curses so that they would know the reason why they were suffering, and the blessings that resulted from obedience. Going back to Daniel's prayer in Daniel chapter 9, you can see that Daniel clearly understood that Judah's captivity was one of the consequences of collective disobedience.

Note, Deuteronomy 28 lists blessings and curses under the law, but there are other "curses" in the Bible that come through disobedience. For example, (a very short list) those who teach rebellion against the Lord. Jeremiah 28:16-17. Those who choose that which God does not delight in. Isaiah 65:11-15. Stubborness and rebellion. I Samuel 15:22-23. Those who add or take away from the word. Revelation 22: 18-19. "Cursed *be* he that doeth the work of the LORD deceitfully, and cursed *be* he that keepeth back his sword from blood" (doesn't do battle when he is supposed to). Jeremiah 48:10. There were original curses against man, woman and the serpent described in Genesis 3, and many more curses from disobedience. Read Deuteronomy 27—there's a big list.

Now the third reason: Part of God's purpose for this protective covering and blessing was to prosper and shelter His chosen people to bring forth the Messiah Jesus Who would take away the sins of the world by His own blood, which is the basis of a new covenant. He was saying, hey, don't mess up here, the salvation of the world depends on you regarding the coming Messiah. There is too much at stake here for you to play around. My whole plan of salvation and re-creation of man in My image is My ultimate plan. As Jesus told the Samaritan woman, salvation is of the Jews. John 4:22. While the covenant you have is a means for your protection, prosperity and revelation, it is also a platform and pattern for the new covenant to come through the Messiah Jesus to the whole world. He will fulfill all the law and its sacrifices by His death and resurrection, satisfying God's holiness, divine justice and mercy.

Previously I talked about "generational curses." While "generational curses" conveys the concept of the personal pipeline of the power and penalty of sin in a family line, curses for disobedience is a conceptual overview of the consequences of sin. The Lord had a covenant with His people and these were the terms. It was a general outline for everyone. With the new covenant through the cross and resurrection of Jesus Christ, God's people would be set free from sin and the power of sin on the inside, and therefore, the blessings of obedience would originate from their personal relationship with the Father, through the Son, empowered by the Holy Spirit. I John 5:14-15: "[14] And this is the confidence that we have in him, that, if we ask any thing according to his will, he heareth us: [15] And if we know that he hear us, whatsoever we ask, we know that we have the petitions that we desired of him."

The principle of experiencing sadness, loss, sometimes sickness and disease, death and other negatives for disobedience did not go away when we transitioned into the new covenant through the blood of Jesus, and similarly, obedience opens the door to many blessings. It is a spiritual law, just like the law of gravity. God loves us unconditionally, but does not bless us unconditionally. It is still true that if you jump off of a high roof you are probably going to break some bones, if you survive. It is still true that if you jump into the vortex of sin there are sad results, but through the grace of God's love and redemption the curse can be turned around, sad results lessened, and used for God's glory because of the cross. We're only to jump (in obedience to God) when God says "jump." Otherwise, we are presuming on God's will and grace that He will give us a pass, or keep us from hitting the ground, no matter what we do—well, it's grace after all. That's the same temptation that Satan tried on Jesus, and it attempts to redefine God's love. Luke 4:9-12. There is nothing sloppy about grace. Grace is amazing and came at a high cost.

Sin, its penalties and effects can be reversed. Jesus took the curses of the law on Himself on the cross. Galatians 3:13. Because of the cross, the Lord could surely do something with the "inner person" to "transcend" ("surpass" "excel" in a glorious way) all circumstances, and often change these circumstances. However, it is a fact that many bad results happen because people disobey the will of God and essentially put themselves under the "curse" again, and those bad results and judgments can affect our family lines. Disobedience opens the door to death. We lose the protection, favor and blessing of God by staying out of His will. It affects a lot of people besides the individual engaging in sin. It proves that His word is true, to our sorrow. His covenant and love for His people is so profound and all-encompassing that He will first give us many layers of direction and instruction.

Apostle Robert Henderson generally says, while we have approached the Lord as Father (for ourselves) or Friend (for others), we can also go to him as Judge to be released from judgments from personal or generational disobedience that are hindering destinies, answers to prayer, healings, and more. Imagine you have a judgment against you for $10,000. Mercifully, your brother pays the debt so you owe nothing. That is what the blood of Jesus does for us. He has paid for everything in our lives and generationally so we can be restored, healed, delivered, blessed, and walk into the destiny God has ordained for us. We can go to God the Judge in the court of heaven the basis of the blood of Jesus, because everything has been paid at the cross, and ask that the judgment against us be paid too. For example, pray this: "On the basis of the blood of Jesus, I repent on behalf of myself and the generations before me on both sides of the family, for fraud, or rebellion, or fear, bitterness, violence, or witchcraft or whatever [declare what you think is relevant], that would hinder [my healing, financial prosperity, my destiny, etc.] and ask you forgive me and my family line of these sins and that the judgment and penalties for these sins be released against me because of the blood of Jesus."

Along with this simple explanation I want to express a bigger picture—and the bigger picture is a short lesson in how God deals with people and His people, often simultaneously (all at the same time). The Bible says that the rain falls on the just and the unjust. The sun shines on everyone. God blesses people that don't even know Him, acknowledge Him, or love Him. He even blesses people that hate Him. He gives many gifts in the natural to the whole world, to people personally and in a global sense. These gifts can be abused and wasted, used for the enemy, nevertheless, He gives them. <u>He equips people and the world for life and the continuation of life.</u> Many people because of their life direction and choices are generally blessed and others generally cursed. This is the general premise of God's love for creation.

In a more spiritual sense for the people of God, loved through salvation, the Lord has a hierarchy of communicating with and directing His people, as seen in scripture. He has a hierarchy of rewarding His people on many levels. In the new covenant there is an emphasis on "relationship" and the love and favor that flow from that. The highest levels of such communication may be the gentle nudging, breeze, impression, or revelation of the Holy Spirit to the heart that is in tune with the Lord—the loving heart of the believer who is eager to please, not just obey, the Master. The Lord speaks to us Spirit to spirit, gives impressions, anointings, visitations, dreams and visions, messages, impartations, and prophecies, or just lays His love and presence in and upon us. After all, HE LIVES in us. We have the wonderful love and power of God ministered to us on a daily loving basis—He dwells in us. Jude tells us "keep yourselves in the love of God." Jude 1:21. My translation of this, is to keep yourself in that love relationship with the Lord, experiencing, releasing love to and from Him and to others, which puts us in a place of continual love and favor with Him. Stay in the groove. Love what God loves. Hate what God hates. Make Him Number One in humble submission and adoration. We always must remember that His kingdom transcends the physical world and His blessings are on many levels.

He also directs us and speaks to us in His word. His word is a lamp unto our feet and a light unto our path. Now if we avoid all of the above for a while, He may allow our world to crumble a bit and we experience circumstances and emptiness that drive us to listen more closely. Not saying that this is always the case when we have trials and tests—James 1: "[2] My brethren, count it all joy when ye fall into divers temptations, (the meaning is tests here); [3] Knowing this, that the trying of your faith worketh patience.[4] But let patience have her perfect work, that ye may be perfect and entire, wanting nothing." So tests and trials have purpose in our lives and build us in the faith. However, God does allow things to fall apart if our sin consistently takes us out of His will.

Deuteronomy 28 is a good summary of how God deals with people "in the natural." He was clear with Israel that if they obeyed Him on the basis of His written word, they would be blessed, and if they didn't they would be cursed, and here was how it was going to happen and this is what it would look like. They were to be a visual picture to the world that there's a God and what His love did for them. His extravagant blessing was a sign, just as the favor and love He pours on us is a sign, and His indwelling presence. Understand that these people were not born-again, Spirit-filled, or transformed by the Spirit of God. They had the word, the Law. They (and their neighbors) had to have some pretty concrete evidence before their eyes as to the consequences if they departed from God, and clear blessings when they obeyed. Although we are in the "new covenant" I do believe that for people who have accepted Jesus as their Savior, sin still opens some painful and terrible doors. You can be a believer and use drugs, lose all your possessions and family, and die of an overdose. Being a believer provides a way out and the grace to do it, but there is always choice involved. And in a time of disobedience, I think we can all say, the Lord was there, and even in my sin, He helped me. The Holy Spirit was still ministering to me in the midst of my mistakes. God's grace and mercy pulled me out. The consequences and even humiliation were surely not as bad as they could have been. He restored my soul and put me back into my inheritance as if I had never departed, like the prodigal son, even though the journey home was humbling and painful and it took a pigpen for a turnaround.

So the consequences of disobedience described in the word are a little guideline to the people of God that if we do things His way, the spiritual door of blessing and favor opens and if we don't, the door closes. A lot of people say, well, this was the old covenant. Yes, it is, but the principles of the old covenant are consistent with the general patterns of the new. There is a reward for faithfulness and obedience. Jesus said, if you love Me, you will obey My commandments. John 14:15. Do we really love Him? While grace covers our sins, God still expects repentance and righteousness—the active living out of our obedience and faith in Him for the kingdom of heaven, and all its blessings, fulfillment, relationship and glory to be opened, and we still can experience consequences of sin if we depart from His way. Romans 2:9-10 (TMSG): "If you go against the grain, you get splinters, regardless of which neighborhood you're from, what your parents taught you, what schools you attended. But if you embrace the way God does things, there are wonderful payoffs, again without regard to where you are from or how you were brought up."

We are a heavenly people and the children of Israel were an earthly people. Many of our blessings are heavenly, and we don't just obey so we can get more earthly stuff. God calls us to suffering at times, and deprivation. Believers are persecuted and rejected. Many times testing can even be the means of fulfillment of our destiny, but that is another subject. Yet, we cannot disregard His principles and the connection between obedience and blessings. It is the Father's good pleasure to give us the kingdom. Matthew 7: "[11] If ye then, being evil, know how to give good gifts unto your children, how much more shall your Father which is in heaven give good things to them that ask him?" Psalms 84: "[11] For the LORD God is a sun and shield; The LORD gives grace and glory; No good thing does He withhold from those who walk uprightly." Romans 8: "[32] He who did not spare His own Son but gave Him up for us all, how will He not also, along with Him, freely give us all things?"

However, the Bible goes on to other layers of communication, direction, and God's expression of His character. Remember the description of the Lord in Exodus 34: "[6] And the LORD passed by before him, and proclaimed, The LORD, The LORD God, merciful and gracious, longsuffering, and abundant in goodness and truth,[7] Keeping mercy for thousands, forgiving iniquity and transgression and sin, and that will by no means clear the guilty;". In the New Testament, we see the amazing love of God in the Person of Jesus Christ, full of grace and truth.

If we fail to heed His written word and subsequently experience consequences, He will still warn us—half of the Old Testament is the prophets doing just that. Look at Hosea, Isaiah, Jeremiah, Ezekiel and others. Jesus, the Great Prophet, also had many prophetic warnings. If we fail to respond to the warning, He will allow the results of our sin to test and refine us. If we fail to turn around, He will judge us. But still in the judgment, He will prove His mercy and faithfulness. He proves His faithfulness in a few ways--by showing that His word is true as the results of obedience or disobedience come to pass. This is the truth part of the lesson. When we fall into distress because of our sins and mistakes, He is still there to love us and prove His covenant of love to us. This is the grace part of the lesson. And further if we obey Him, there are rewards, this is also the love part of the message. His story imprinted in the pages of scripture is not just about obedience, it is about love. It's a love story. God wants a loving family relationship. That is His highest desire. It's a family story, a new family story after Adam botched the first family story. Just look at the book of Ruth, where the original players (Naomi and her family) disregarded the covenant (and 3 out of 4 died and Naomi was left impoverished), but God restored everyone beautifully through a lowly Gentile woman named Ruth who married her (willing) kinsman redeemer, Boaz. In fact, the whole world is blessed for eternity because Boaz redeemed and married Ruth. Their descendants include King David and the Lord Jesus Christ Himself.

The last step, and I really don't believe this is reserved for believers, but in a global sense, a world that has failed to respond to God's grace, truth or judgments, then the wrath of God comes. He is no longer dealing with the world (which already is not in covenant) in terms of redemption, but wrath as an expression of His holy character. Look at the book of Revelation. People who turn their back on God, eventually experience the wrath of God because you cannot kick God out of the world, you can only reject and cut yourself off from the love of His Son, Jesus Christ. When people turn their back on God, they are really turning their back on Jesus Christ, our Mediator (Go-between), Who has taken the blows for us. They are rejecting the only One who can give them mercy—people are so blinded. I do not believe true believers will experience the wrath of God, but we will all be accountable for what we have done or not done.

There are many examples in the word of the consequences of disobedience. The curses resulting from disobedience can be stopped in our lives by the power of the blood of Jesus. This is not to say that we will avoid every consequence of our sins and those of the generations before us, but the Lord can intervene and give us a new future with the joys of His presence and new blessings. Jesus reverses the curse by His death on the cross. Everything ends and begins at the cross. Notice that many of the curses listed in Deuteronomy 28 affect future generations. How do we turn this around? Repent of course, for the kingdom of heaven is at hand. God doesn't enjoy our pain, but pain is a big motivator. The Bible also says in Proverbs 26:2 that a "curse causeless shall not come." When we stay under the protection of the Almighty through the blood of Jesus and walk in obedience and knowledge, curses in this context do not have access. When we close our own "open doors" of disobedience, and close them generationally, there is no legal right of entry.

So Deuteronomy 28 is a little motivational lesson to listen to the Lord and do it His way, because there are always consequences. The Bible isn't a fantasy book; it is stone cold reality. It took the death of Jesus Christ, the Son of God, to turn things around, and His resurrection to give us a new identity and life. It will take cataclysmic events in heaven and on earth, judgments and shakings, to finally implement the breaking of the curses and effects of sin originating in the Garden of Eden and continuing through man's disobedient history. But for the meanwhile, we can abide in the secret place of the most High under the shadow of the Almighty, that is, under the shadow of the cross and covered by His blood.

3. Curses spoken from others

Remember that words have power. Remember it operates as a curse if a child was always called stupid, or slow, or a failure, or ugly, or clumsy. Such spoken curses need to be broken in the name of Jesus, and the blessings of God, planted like new plants in the soil of the heart. Pull out the weeds of false identity, put in the seeds of what God says about us as believers: We are accepted in the beloved, we have the mind of Christ, we are the apple of His eye, I can do all things through Christ who strengthens me, and others. Many Christians will cram the Word into their heads and hearts, and try to live by it, only to find it hasn't taken root properly, because the scripture is so crowded by weeds of the past, an emotional history, that needs to be rewritten page by page by the blood of Jesus. That is why good soil is so important for the life of God to grow. The ground needs to be cleared of weeds, the lies uprooted, broken up (repentance and forgiveness), moistened with the dew of the Holy Spirit, fertilized (by dying to self), and planted with the new Word of God so Christ may grow in us. It is quite a process and by no means overnight. There are "suddenlies," but that is because of the steady growth of the life of God in our hearts.

Spoken words of curse need to be broken in the believer's life. Such words are limitations and bondages which dwarf growth and block wholeness. Words that put-down, ridicule, and suppress a person should be broken. Anything that has bent us from our true stature should be cast down and broken. We curse ourselves by our inner faith in the negative, rather than what God says about us. But it is not like we can just "snap out of it." There are attitudes and emotions that must be affirmatively dealt with by the power of the blood of Jesus and the Holy Spirit, and replaced with godly principles. Emotional history needs to be sanctified—in other words, made holy by releasing our experiences and attitudes to God for deliverance, healing, restoration, and then divine order.

Now I am talking very generally here, but I want you to get the concept. The curse, "you're stupid" will be enforced by spirits which disable the individual from thinking or acting clearly. Other confusion, lies, and uncleanness, whether emotional attitudes or spirits, "join the club" so to speak, such as low self-esteem, self-rejection, self-hatred, rebellion, anger, violence, self-destructive activity, mental passivity. Look at what might happen: A person may be blocked from learning, because of a spoken curse, no matter how intelligent they truly are. This curse and any demonic enforcers will attract further curses of the same variety. And time will be spent around persons broken and abused in similar ways. Ungodly habits develop. Life is stifled and opportunities lost—maybe one result is prison instead of an education leading to a future. Lives are limited instead of expanded. That is why the gospel is the great liberating force on the planet and there is so much warfare against the truth. That is why we must understand these principles for freedom, or we will drift into the effects and bondage of the forces arrayed against us without even thinking.

Satan separates people and segregates them according to their sins and weaknesses. Failure may enter in, and a lifetime of brokenness is a result. The curse can easily run to the next generation. Parents can abuse their children in the ways they have been abused, whether consciously or not. Those who have not experienced the redemptive love of Jesus in any depth can unknowingly transfer who they are to the next generation. Having been blocked from expansion and growth, these blockages may be transferred to the next generation resulting in dysfunctional areas in families. When pain occurs due to rejection and failure, tragically the frustration could be addressed through violence and anger, or withdrawal and passivity. Drugs, alcohol, or other forms of escape only numb the senses, and deal with pain in a false manner, reinforcing denial of the true problem. These all bear fruit of sin and reproduce more sin.

The child called "stupid" however, probably does not suffer isolated offenses. There are usually cumulative offenses by parent(s), caretakers, or other close relatives. More realistically the spoken word of curse on the child is one of the fruits of the heart attitude of anger, rejection, frustration, abuse, insensitivity of the persons with whom he/she is in close relationship. As I said earlier, Jesus told us not to offend the little ones or cause them to stumble. It would better for a millstone to be placed around your neck and you be cast into the sea, than to cause a little one to stumble. Offenses will come, Jesus said. However, He warns us not to be the offender. Hardness of heart passes from generation to generation. Those who have been hardened by their own experience of offenses cannot always respond in softness or wholeness to children. So a child who starts with a tender heart, a heart potentially open to God, has his or her heart changed from a heart of flesh to a heart of stone. Only through the new birth and the transforming power of the Holy Spirit can the heart of stone then be changed back into a heart of flesh.

As Ezekiel wrote of the Lord's work of transformation: "I will take away the stony heart out of your flesh, and I will give you a heart of flesh." Ezekiel 36:26. What a huge work—it took the cross. Sin and the offenses from others change human beings into rocks. Our inherited sin nature makes the human soul vulnerable to this deadening process as we do not have within us the nature of God to innately respond in love and forgiveness (or in a divine dimension of love and forgiveness), nor do we have the spiritual resources to set ourselves or others free. So the old nature retrenches and grows defensive, hurt, and mistrusting. It puts up walls, and eases pain through, probably, sinful habits and family line patterns of escape and distraction. To remedy this, we must be born again and grow in God, whereby we can have a new heart, new mind and new will. That is the only true life. Now Jesus the Chief Cornerstone must become the new "Rock" in our lives which is no longer based on a hardened heart, the rock of sin. We move from a dead foundation, to the Chief Cornerstone of life, Jesus the Rock, so we may become living stones. We need to be transformed by the renewing of our minds. But this is not just our thinking process but emotional patterns stored in our minds and bodies and hearts.

Look, you do not need to be a therapist or psychologist to understand or minister inner healing and deliverance, you basically need to be led of the Holy Spirit, as you examine your heart or when you minister to others. The Holy Spirit is the Spirit of Truth and will guide you into all truth. That is not to negate the value of such professions. A great deal can be learned with a therapist or psychologist or educating yourself on a subject as you navigate your soul with the Holy Spirit—a great deal. And perhaps such help will be illuminating in your journey. But in the end, the Holy Spirit is your guide and the Holy Spirit has the power for true and lasting freedom and healing. You are enabled by the powerful gifts and revelation of the Holy Spirit to minister to yourself or others. The Lord knew this and desired this when He gave the Holy Spirit to everyone in His body, not just leaders. The Holy Spirit will have God's timing and direction for your healing and deliverance. You know historically and practically what you have experienced and what your family has experienced. That is the starting point. God knows how to get to these places and bring His new life, and in what order.

For example, I was talking to a woman once (not even ministering) and I kept getting the name "Frances, Frances, Frances." Finally, I asked her what "Frances" meant to her. She said her name was originally Frances, but her father had an affair when she was around three years old with a woman by the name of Frances, and so her mother changed her name to something else. However, a disruption had taken place in her soul which the Lord wanted to remedy. The gifts of the Holy Spirit were in operation. First, the word of knowledge was operating as I got the name "Frances" in my spirit, and then gifts of healing were in operation as a friend of mine and I ministered to her emotions. Sometimes the Lord will show me (or another person ministering with me, as we often work in teams back and forth receiving revelation) that an individual has been sexually abused or had an abortion or been rejected by father or mother. Obviously the Holy Spirit wants to deal with the highlighted area. Maybe a dozen other areas need restoration or deliverance, but follow what the Holy Spirit emphasizes. Sometimes you start in one area, and then a person's history just unfolds for healing and deliverance. This is just to say, the Holy Spirit is the Supreme Professional, and we are following His lead. Additionally, because of the holiness of God and the power of His love and presence, there is a dimension of healing and deliverance that can never come from just professionals in this world. Deliverance, inner healing and restoration all have a supernatural and divine dimension. It is the Son Who sets us free.

Again, the kingdom of heaven has a different "operating system" than the world's systems.

This does not mean that we never pray in simple methodical ways. Often I ask a person to go through some general repentance prayers that are applicable to their life, or break generational curses, or break judgments against the person. These lay the groundwork for further deliverance and healing. But as we pray and interact the doors open up.

Now, getting back to personal curses: A prime example of such a curse is seen in the life of Jabez. 1 Chronicles 4:9 - 10 (KJV) "⁹And Jabez was more honorable than his brethren: and his mother called his name Jabez, saying, Because I bare him with sorrow. ¹⁰And Jabez called on the God of Israel, saying, Oh that thou wouldest bless me indeed, and enlarge my coast, and that thine hand might be with me, and that thou wouldest keep *me* from evil, that it may not grieve me! And God granted him that which he requested."

In other words, she gave her son the name "pain" because she "bore him with sorrow." Perhaps his birth had been very painful, or the circumstances surrounding his birth had brought her pain, or perhaps she did not want another child. We do not know. But from the scripture we do know that Jabez didn't like what his mother had done, and he called on God, his Father, to change his destiny from a curse to a blessing. I don't see a natural father around in this story helping Jabez or his mother. Maybe his absence or behavior was part of the pain, but the message is clear that we can call on our Heavenly Father to change things. His mother had transferred all of her anguish and problems to her child. Such "transference" happens all the time, and he was the scapegoat for her pain. It was a selfish maneuver on her part by a woman in denial (didn't want to face her own issues). Let Jabez deal with the pain, it's not my fault. Jabez is the problem. Downgrade and disregard Jabez, and I don't have to look at myself. Let him be the cause of all our hurts for the family. His brothers didn't help either. He had lived with a name and destiny from birth that was destructive, and no one was helping him find a higher or better life.

But Jabez was a young man of faith and he acted alone in faith. Not wanting his destiny set by his mother or anyone else, he sought a higher and better destiny: God's blessing, an enlargement of his life, God's hand upon him, and protection from evil, that it would not grieve him. Pain limits life, we become prisoners of the past, but blessing enlarges life, we live for what God has designed for the future. Jabez represents the symbolic struggle that we all face. We call on the God of the cross to bring us out of the old painful declarations and memories from our families or the preceding generations and move into newness of life and the Lord's blessings by faith in the word.

Other people may call us something, but it cannot stick unless we let it—this is a relatively easy level to uproot. It is more destructive when we may think of ourselves in a negative light, consider ourselves stupid or worthless, unattractive, bad, damaged goods, wrong, or failures—see the sections in this book on personal curses, and inner vows covenants and negative core beliefs. Unfortunately, a lot of these attitudes are absorbed into our minds, bodies and emotions almost unconsciously. We become a storage unit that no one has the energy to clean out, rather than a living person. I did not originate the term, "negative core beliefs," but it is used to describe what we think about ourselves, life in general, attitudes about other people, in a negative way, that is almost unconscious. Negative core beliefs may be, I am always a failure, I don't deserve love, it is not safe to trust people, I'm inferior, nobody listens to me, life is unfair, I am undesirable, nobody loves me, I've always been sick or weak, happiness never lasts so I should reject it, you're on your own, I have to manipulate people because I cannot get what I want otherwise, and hundreds of other beliefs. Perhaps the generation before you communicated the message in one way or another, "toughen up, don't show any emotions, it is a sign of weakness." All these beliefs can pass through families. This is the message that runs like background noise, without people even realizing it. But these messages create disharmony with God's intended promise and plan for our lives. Like background noise, we become so used to it, we don't even notice it after a while.

Curses may be spoken over a child, for example, in anger or abuse, and usually this happens from those who are closest to the child. But God can turn around all the curses, even the family tragedies. Calling on God the Father can "father" something new in us by the power of the Holy Spirit. Jabez was redeemed from the curse of his mother, a natural line curse, and a destiny she had tried to set for him, by calling on the blessing of his Father God, a spiritual line blessing. By the power of the blood of Jesus we can speak in the name of Jesus to break the curses, destinies and patterns that have been spoken over our lives, and release a blessing in the name of Jesus. Some of these curses are very deep and may lie hidden for years, but the Holy Spirit can and will reveal secrets.

4. Witchcraft Curses and Occult Practices

Witchcraft curses, spells, incantations, psychic, "soulish" or demonic prayers spoken by people who operate in the occult, hexes, vexes, Santeria, voodoo, and other occult practices, are a huge realm of spiritual power outside of the word of God. I am going to include in this segment, prayers to gods other than God the Father in the name of Jesus. People who utilize spells and curses, for example, will say some are good and some are bad. People can use spiritual power to heal diseases, manipulate events for prosperity, pray to gods of their choosing expecting a result (and maybe getting the desired result). There are many spiritual systems out there with a lot of power; it is just that any spiritual system not based on the Father, Son and Holy Spirit, the Word of God, the blood of Jesus and the power of the Holy Spirit, is not of God. God is holy, the rest are not. He is the God of creation and salvation—the blood of Jesus "sanctifies" us or makes us holy to be like our holy Father God with the right to approach Him and be in fellowship with Him. Without holiness no one can see God—so whatever people are tapping into, it isn't God. Hebrews 12:14. Whether the result would be considered "good" by someone, or "bad" by someone, it does not originate from God (the real God), and therefore is from the tree of the knowledge of good and evil, not the tree of life.

We live in a spiritual universe, but not all spirits are of God. The apostle John writes in I John 4 "[1] Beloved, believe not every spirit, but try the spirits whether they are of God: because many false prophets are gone out into the world. [2] Hereby know ye the Spirit of God: Every spirit that confesseth that Jesus Christ is come in the flesh is of God: [3] And every spirit that confesseth not that Jesus Christ is come in the flesh is not of God: and this is that spirit of antichrist, whereof ye have heard that it should come; and even now already is it in the world." Our relationship with God is a holy one, because the blood of Jesus cleanses us, and gives us the right and power to go to the throne room of God and heaven by His grace. We are a heavenly people. No matter how any spiritual system is characterized, it is out of the will and revelation of God if it is not based on the Lord Jesus Christ, His death for the salvation of the world through the shedding of His blood as the eternal sacrifice for our sins, and His resurrection.

Let's just say that a curse or hex or soulish prayer is sent your way, or someone includes you and your future in a prayer to some other god. These have power to influence our circumstances, cause oppression, confusion, strife, manipulate, release sickness, create havoc in a family or church, or create bondage. However, the first thing to remember (if you discern something sent in your direction causing you to feel oppressed, creating confusion, or under a cloud, etc.), is that THE BLOOD OF JESUS IS MORE POWERFUL! Stay under the blood of Jesus. Come against and break any curse or spoken word sent against you or your loved ones, by the power of the blood of Jesus and in the name of Jesus. These can be disorienting, so get back on your spiritual feet by prayer and warfare. Check your heart too. Stay in obedience and be quick to forgive and repent, so that no open doors are supplied to the enemy. Ask the Lord to show you any open doors or how to do spiritual warfare more effectively if you detect interference.

Plead the blood of Jesus over your life, circumstances, family, friends and whatever else the Lord shows you daily. The blood of Jesus is more powerful than anything the enemy can send your way or even well-meaning people who are not operating according to the will of God. I don't want Christians to pray for me out of the will of God. Don't give me some prophetic word that is not consistent with what the Holy Spirit witnesses to me. These can cause confusion or oppression. Have some spiritual discernment. There are also Christians who say things and project dreams about your future, that are out of line with the will of God. Just break these projections and keep moving. But with regard to the deliberate occult hexes, curses, incantations etc., all the power of these methods of manipulation, control, destruction, entrapment, are nothing compared to the blood of Jesus. I am sure there are mysterious intricacies in all of these types of spoken words and curses, but they are no match for our God. I don't want any demons released in my direction.

How do you break a curse? Very simple, "I break this curse against me or words attached to me in the name of the Lord Jesus Christ. I come against this curse by the blood of Jesus Christ. I bind and break the power of every demon sent against me, and command it to be bound, leave me and go into the dry places in the name of Jesus." Some people have suggested affirmatively sending curses back "with judgment to repentance." In other words, let the person doing the cursing experience the effect of the curse themselves to bring them to repentance—like a spiritual boomerang. That may be the only thing that wakes them up. I would be led of the Holy Spirit on this. The Bible also says pray for those who despitefully use you and persecute you. Pray for their salvation and deliverance. People need to understand there is an automatic boomerang effect from a curse; that curse can return back to the sender, maybe not in the same form, but in oppression and bondage on their life. Psalms 109: "[17]As he loved cursing, so let it come unto him: as he delighted not in blessing, so let it be far from him."

Remember there are people out there that hate Jesus Christ, hate the people of God, hate the love, truth and holiness of God on earth, want to destroy, oppress and curse God's people, stop His great commission from going forth and stop Jesus Christ, King of Kings, from ruling and reigning on this earth. There are spiritual principalities that want the whole planet under bondage. The prince of the power of the air works in the children of disobedience, (Ephesians

2:2), so it is not quietly neutral out there. Get into some warfare as well on a daily basis.

There are also many people that couldn't care less about our holy God and operate in a different (albeit false) spiritual universe. It seems "spiritual" but it is not of God. Our spiritual universe is built on Jesus, the cross, resurrection, new life through His blood, the Word of God, the will of the Father and the power of the Holy Spirit. There are people who try to manipulate and control other people by occult powers. Sometimes they may even think it is good. However, it is not good if it is not of God. If you belong to Jesus, no weapon formed against you can prosper, and any tongue that rises up in judgment against you will be condemned. Isaiah 54:17. You have the power and authority to stop anything against you or your family or church, or to escalate it even more, city or nation, by the power of the blood of Jesus and the name of Jesus.

These "prayers," curses, incantations, hexes and other spoken declarations release unclean spirits to accomplish the intent of the curse. It is a curse, because it is spoken, accesses a spiritual source other than God, and the demon is released to bring to pass what is intended in the spoken word. The fancy, convoluted words are just releasing demons. Conversely, when we speak the word of God, the Spirit of God and the angels of God are released to produce God's result. Even when we pray for people as Christians, it is important to discern and then pray the will and timing of God for that person. We can pray with the tongues of men and angels, and in the utterance of the Holy Ghost.

In general, there is no such thing as good witchcraft or good occult powers, or good new age meditation, or good hexes—you eventually reap a problem because scripture is clear that we reap what we sow, and these powers do not originate from the Father, Son and Holy Ghost. That includes all prayers to any god other than Father God, in the name of the Son, Jesus Christ, no matter how nice the people are or how good the prayer. Those who are involved in the occult will reap a crop of confusion, spiritual darkness, and many other problems for generations. Witchcraft and accessing or opening oneself to any occult source is like spiritual cement. It keeps the will and mercy of God away, and holds its participants in covenants of death, covenants with demons, and covenants with unbelievers, all of which need to be broken. There is no such thing as living the good *lie*. There are problems in many areas for people accessing this power, reaching to their descendants—sickness, poverty, oppression, sexual uncleanness, family breakdown, mental illness, early death, and more.

Let's say out of ignorance, curiosity, impatience, stupidity, or deception, you went to a fortune teller, palm reader, dialed a psychic and got a "prophetic word," or got some information or answer on a Ouija board, tea leaves, astrological chart or tarot cards. First of all, you have allowed yourself to be cursed, because such practices are against scripture and do not originate from the true God—no matter how good or accurate they may seem. Second, demons have been released in your direction to bring the "word" or answer to pass. And third, you have set in motion something that is destructive to your life, and generations following. What you need to do: Repent for accessing such means of information, renounce the practice, and break the power of the curse on your life because of the sin. Next, bind and cast out any demon that has been released, and send that spirit to the dry places in Jesus' name. You have opened a door and it is not a good one. You want to close it. Again, I don't want anything that seems "good" if it is not from God. On a slightly different note, stay away from the "wonderful" vibes of meditation and yoga. Do you know where they are coming from? Each yoga position is offered to Hindu gods, and therefore an open door for the demonic. Only the Spirit of God is holy. Just because you experience some peace or have a supernatural experience in your soul realm does not mean you are a "spiritual" person or you have accessed the Spirit of God. You are accessing something, but not the Holy Spirit.

Finally, just as an aside or clarification, I hear many people say they are spiritual but not religious. The whole concept is a false comparison. First, unless we are born again, we are spiritually dead. It's that simple. Second, Jesus didn't call people to be "religious" He called them to be holy and follow Him. To me, any person who makes such a statement is either ignorant of the true and Living God; has experienced something of a spiritual nature in their soul realm; does not want to commit in obedience to God; or, best case scenario, hungers for something of God but has not found the truth.

But the good news is, that power of the blood of Jesus and the name of Jesus and the power of the Holy Spirit, can break the power of any curses. They are no match. Just break them. Know also that your interest or even vulnerability in that area may hearken back generationally.

5. Personal curses.

A little more on this—these may be curses we speak over ourselves or believe about ourselves in an almost unconscious monologue—I'll never be good enough, I'll never measure up, I'm bad, I'm ashamed, I can't do this or that. I am calling them curses, because they are an inner monologue in opposition to the image, likeness and will of God for His children through Jesus Christ—these are not the meditations of the new creation. The scripture says in Psalms 19: "[14] Let the words of my mouth, and the meditation of my heart, be acceptable in thy sight, O LORD, my strength, and my redeemer." That goes for our inner thoughts about who we are, among other things—do our thoughts line up with God's thoughts towards us as revealed in the word? Such curses are often hidden in our hearts from the pain, neglect or trauma we may have experienced when we were young. They may often be the undercurrent of our actions, working on the level of deep emotional patterns that we don't even realize—some passed from generations before us. They direct the ship of our lives without us even being aware of their influence and we wonder why we shipwreck in the same ways over and over again. When there is no light, we stumble on things we don't even know about. Proverbs 4:19 says the way of the wicked is as darkness: they know not at what they stumble. But Jesus said in John 11: "[9] If any man walk in the day, he stumbleth not, because he seeth the light of this world." Being set free from these curses requires a determined desire to see what is in our own hearts and then submit such attitudes to God, allowing them to be replaced with the truth of the word of God. Often our hearts are so trained in failure or sadness, for example, it may take a while to be cleansed—and some of this is generational. David cried, "Create in me a clean heart, O God, and renew a right spirit within me." Psalms 51:10-11. Thankfully, many times the Holy Spirit simply overrides our inner judgments against ourselves, and substitutes the truth of the new creation in Christ.

In line with personal curses are vows that operate as curses—I'll never trust again, I will not give. These types of inner vows limit our blessings. I won't enter into relationship with this or that type of person. I'll never try to do this or that again. I will cover more on this later. Break these vows and be sensitive when they arise again.

And a big stumbling stone—shame. Shame is so powerful, we don't even know it is there, but it affects every area of our lives. Shame is a killer, and will try and take over as a covering of our souls, if we let it. Shame comes when we think we are unworthy, unclean, damaged goods, we have sinned, or made life altering mistakes. Shame can be generational—the people before us felt shame, through discrimination, massive trauma, abuse, fear, poverty, personal mistakes, failure and other reasons. Shame has its own hidden history. Folks, Jesus took our shame, so are you being righteous by keeping it? He doesn't want us bowed down by it. The enemy would prefer we felt shame all the time. It is a hard covering to break and becomes part of our personality. Be determined not to carry the curse that the enemy is forced to carry for eternity. It's not ours. Shame goes to the core of our being and who we are, whereas guilt can be related to specific acts. Sometimes shame is passed through generations. The father, mother, grandparents felt shame and so it naturally falls on us—everyone feels inferior or victimized. But we must operate supernaturally here. It is not ours to carry.

In conclusion, several types of curses can negatively impact our lives: Generational curses, curses from others, curses we speak over ourselves or meditate upon in our hearts, curses from disobedience, and occult curses. Being cleansed from curses is another layer of cleansing that we need. Curses can hinder us, no matter how much we want to move forward. Remember Jesus became a curse for us.

FOURTH LEVEL: SOUL TIES

The fourth level of cleansing is breaking ungodly soul ties. I am going to include in this overall term, associated spiritual connections as well. These are emotional ties that bind us and that originate from connections that are outside the will of God. Notice that they are "ungodly" soul ties. There can be soul ties to inanimate objects, substances, places, animals, people, sounds, and smells—not all are ungodly, but breaking ungodly soul ties gives us freedom.

Again, not all soul ties are ungodly. Soul ties are necessary and important in life. God intends us to be connected, be a part of something and joined in godly relationships with others. He is a relational God. The Lord wants us to belong to Himself first, to family, to spouses, to the body of Christ, to friends, even to nations, and peoples—there is a plan in all of it. Belonging and connection is built into us as created beings. Our hearts were designed to love and be loved, and to be mutually engaged in life with each other. It is not good that man or woman be alone. When Jesus was baptized at the Jordan River, the Father said, "This is My beloved Son in Whom I am well pleased." The Father identified Jesus as His beloved Son— the ultimate in affection and belonging. It is the character and desire of God. Matthew 3:17. Although God wants us to "belong" and "belonging" is built into us, our connections are not meant to be more important than our relationship with the Lord, and His will and principles. He is our primary and supreme connection. However, without connections we will "be longing" for the comfort and support of belonging for long time.

The Lord instituted the covenant of marriage whereby two people become one flesh—literally a new creation is formed. Clearly the Lord intends soul ties in such a covenantal relationship. The Lord established the "body of Christ" in which we are to be joined together with different functions. Paul writes in Colossians 2:2 – 3 "²My goal is that they will be encouraged and knit together by strong ties of love. I want them to have full confidence because they have complete understanding of God's secret plan, which is Christ himself.

[3]In him lie hidden all the treasures of wisdom and knowledge." He desires the hearts of His people to be knit together in love. Ephesians 4: "[4] *There is* one body, and one Spirit, even as ye are called in one hope of your calling."

We have friendships, human associations, work and business relationships and godly associations. We love our pets. But the Bible makes it clear that we are to be careful with whom (or with what) we become attached and to keep in the boundaries of covenant and/or obedience and not to get into idolatry. Most of all, God want to set us free to <u>cleave to Him</u> and be the persons we were created to be, not stretched out, scattered like debris, and owned by others. Jesus is in the center of you and me.

Let's look at ungodly soul ties for a while. Why are ungodly soul ties so important in terms of deliverance? The reason is because we can be attached to people or places or objects that control us, bring pain or pleasure out of the will of God, and transfer demons, among other things. They can keep us in bondage. Furthermore, our focus is taken off of the Lord God as our primary love and a type of idolatry takes place. You don't have to be with a person physically for transference of spirits. The soul tie can also hold in hurt, pain, lust or fear, pleasure, confusion, death or trauma, for example, that should be gone.

Some people are tied to money. For example, the rich young ruler described in the Bible had money as his god; he was not free to follow Jesus. Achan, the Troubler of Israel, was attached to a garment and a piece of gold. He took something that belonged to the devil, the garment, and something that belonged to God, the piece of gold. It hurt the whole nation. Joshua 7: 20-21.

Some people are tied to needles and pipes, music, pictures, letters, pornography. You can have soul ties to your favorite entertainment, certain music, electronic devices, car, clothes, jewelry, name brand alcohol, drugs, and anything else. While it is important to break the ungodly ties, it is equally important to repent for the attachment and seek the root of the damage that may have allowed such an attachment. Objects can give legal ground for demonic oppression—documents, agreements, gifts, clothes, pictures from ex-boyfriends, or girlfriends, sexual partners of any variety, or any electronic communication—and there are so many varieties now, can be a channel for the enemy. We are dealing with social networking sites and apps now, and all these can be shoveling in the enemy's lies, transferring spirits and creating bondage. Our minds, spirits, emotions will be a lot less tied in an ungodly manner, if we get rid of this baggage. Some soul ties occur when a person has been molested or raped. It was not a desired tie, but the soul is nevertheless bound in a negative and destructive bondage to the person who was the perpetrator. If there is no deliverance, the cycle can even be repeated, and sorrow becomes a way of life. Add to this is the shame involved and reluctance to speak about the violation.

With soul ties can be covenants that are ungodly. The ungodly covenants of joining a gang or occult organization, can be controlling for life. I will also include religious or semi-religious systems that are not based on the word of God, such as the Masons or Mormons—there are many more. In such a case, break the covenant (even blood covenant) with that gang or group and any vows, and enter into the blood covenant with the Lord Jesus Christ. The enemy can't have you. The blood of Jesus is stronger than any other blood covenant. For example: "I break this blood covenant now with XXX in the name of Jesus Christ, and I join myself to Jesus Christ by covenant through the blood He shed on the cross." "I break every covenant with death. I break every covenant with [such and such] person [or system] that was not of you." "I break all my vows and covenants with XXX organization." You may have to go through a list of vows you have made. Let the Holy Spirit be your guide. Break ungodly coverings. Some covenants are over. Perhaps a spouse has died, or there has been a divorce because of infidelity. I would go ahead and break those covenants spiritually as well. You would be surprised the liberation one receives. Time to move on. That does not mean that you stop loving, it just means that you are cutting any residual trailers of being bound. Because of our soul ties with people, and what we experience with them, we can actually be tied to sadness, loss, pain. It is almost as if we have covenants of sadness, loss or pain, because we are gaining something out of it, trading wholeness for the comfort of remembrance. It is a little familiar safe space, but it is destructive, and must be renounced.

Perhaps someone is sexually abused and they are threatened that they must "vow" never to tell anyone, or you have created have a self-imposed vow—it is time to break these vows and connected soul ties as well.

Some people are attached through sin to others, and so even though they may want to be free, the attachment through sin is strong and demonic spirits continue to transfer even after the relationship may be over. These can be ties related to using drugs or alcohol with another person, and anything else. There can be ties in pornography. Of course, there are very strong ties in sexual relations or sexual exposure that includes imaginary sex. That is one reason the Bible clearly tells us to "flee fornication" and that fornication is a sin against one's own body.

A person can have ties to alternate personalities, personas, pleasures, or the people of the past, so that when pressure, problems, hunger, physical and emotional, loneliness or boredom come, it is easy to revert back to these things. They become a "default" pattern.

Everything has a payoff. We have to ask the question: What is the soul tie feeding? It is clear that the Lord would want to break these things that diminish the capacity of our hearts to love God, so that His people can go on to a greater life. Whatever we gain outside of God's boundaries and commandments is not an exchange worth making. Renounce them and move onto an authentic life in Christ. We can't be bigger people with smaller attachments. Proverbs 4: "[23] Keep your heart with all diligence, for out of it *spring* the issues of life." What fills our hearts is what we are going to live by, whether consciously or not. Breaking the ungodly ties allows the Lord to work and help us grow.

The Lord, the people around us that God has placed in our lives, the paths He has called us to walk and our destiny in Him, the body of Christ, and a hurting dying world deserve our undivided attention. And if a person's attention is on connections that are not of

God, then we are cheating God, cheating ourselves, and cheating others.

Furthermore, in ministering deliverance it may be required to break soul ties between a believer and an object to obtain freedom from a third party or demonic entity. Sometimes in deliverance, people need to take off jewelry, because of soul ties associated with that jewelry, or that jewelry has an occult or ungodly symbolic configuration that allows transference of spirits or blocks the deliverance. Perhaps you are trying to pray for someone and they are wearing a pentagram. I would ask the person to take off the piece of jewelry.

It is always important to break soul ties with past ungodly sexual relationships—whether you can remember them all or not, and with all fantasy sex. If you had sexual relations, or a sexual experience, with someone outside of God's definition of marriage, that soul tie is out of the will of God, and it has to be broken. Such ties are outside of God's covenant, and therefore cannot be blessed. If you married the person later, break the earlier ties that were sinful. Even in godly covenants there may be parts of the relationship that exert ungodly control. These need to be broken, so that the relationship can flourish in the will of God. Perhaps there is a type of manipulation in a marriage. That needs to be broken, knowledge of overcoming realized, and restoration in godly boundaries claimed. Call back your soul that has been broken and scattered and command the other person's soul or any fragments thereof to leave. Please see Appendix E as well for Renunciation of Sexual Sins.

With ungodly soul ties, individuals may feel bonded to someone they do not even like, or feel connected to the wrong person to meet their needs, or someone who is clearly destructive to them—note how many people put up with abuse. In cases of abuse, a person's will gets so battered, the internal strength to be free is greatly diminished. Such ties can hinder a person's ability to move onto a godly relationship because the individual is dominated by another person. The knitting together of our souls with another person means that either party can exercise great control. Individuals may feel bonded to something they don't want or like as well.

Also, pornography provides strong soul ties and demonic ties. When these ties are broken then there is space for genuine covenantal relationships. Because pornography introduces demons to the viewer/participant, and can actually change a person physiologically, like any real sexual encounter, it will take some repentance, renunciation, and healing to be free. So, if you have soul ties with pornographic images, those ties need to be broken and then command the demons to leave. What will your life be like without pornography to fill the gap? FREE!

Ungodly control is exerted in many relationships and can be enforced by evil spirits. When we break soul ties in deliverance, it may also be valuable to cast out spirits of control from the other person. Whenever there are sexual relations with another person, the soul tie that is created has the potential to exert great influence, even if it simply reinforces internal destructive patterns. With all soul ties there is possible transference of spirits. When emotions are open, or there is a vulnerability through sin, spirits can transfer. In ungodly sexual relationships, not only may a person get sexually transmitted disease(s), but sexually transmitted demons.

1 Corinthians 6:15–20 (NKJV): "15Do you not know that your bodies are members of Christ? Shall I then take the members of Christ and make *them* members of a harlot? Certainly not! 16Or do you not know that he who is joined to a harlot is one body *with her?* For *"the two,"* He says, *"shall become one flesh."* 17But he who is joined to the Lord is one spirit *with Him.* 18Flee sexual immorality. Every sin that a man does is outside the body, but he who commits sexual immorality sins against his own body. 19Or do you not know that your body is the temple of the Holy Spirit *who is* in you, whom you have from God, and you are not your own? 20For you were bought at a price; therefore glorify God in your body and in your spirit, which are God's."

The Bible says that we become one person in a sexual relationship. When the relationship ends, there is a tearing of your soul. In the old days, people would commonly say, this person broke my heart, or it is hard to pull away from that person. In such ungodly relationships, our souls become fragmented and broken, and that is why we must break the ties that are ungodly and ask the Lord to restore our souls. In this confused world with multiple "hook-ups" accessed through any number of dating apps, streaming porn, even robots, casual sex, the driven sexuality of some lifestyles, the damage to souls is enormous, even if this means nothing to the participants but instantaneous gratification. Our bodies are to be the temple of the Holy Ghost—that is part of our salvation, preserved for a holy and covenantal union in marriage. God is here to forgive and restore, even remake relationships into His image, but He also wills to cleanse and separate individuals from ungodly acts. For example, consider a husband who has had many sexual contacts in earlier years. A bit of his soul is attached to this woman (or man), a bit to another, and so on. I do not believe faithfulness will be easy in the marriage. Such ties need to be broken in the name of Jesus, and any unclean spirits that have entered in and through the relationship, commanded to leave, as well as a layer by layer cleansing and healing of the mind, will, and emotions. Then focus can be restored to the spouse, giving emotional, spiritual, and physical energy where God has sanctioned. Sexual relations provide tremendous vulnerability to transference of spirits.

Solomon was a man with many soul ties. I Kings 11:1-11 shows us how the soul ties in his life took his heart away from the Living God. 1 Kings 11:1 – 3 (NLT): "¹Now King Solomon loved many foreign women. Besides Pharaoh's daughter, he married women from Moab, Ammon, Edom, Sidon, and from among the Hittites. ²The LORD had clearly instructed his people not to intermarry with those nations, because the women they married would lead them to worship their gods. Yet Solomon insisted on loving them anyway. ³He had seven hundred wives and three hundred concubines." As scripture describes, all these ungodly relationships took his heart away from the Lord. Solomon was a man with great compulsion and bondage, that really had more power than all his wisdom. Given his choices, it is clear he discarded the wisdom God gave him—what he petitioned to have in prayer—to serve his flesh. Consider Sampson under the control of Delilah. It cost him his life. That manipulative spirit in her, his attraction to her, and his soul ties to her, finished him—even when he knew she was dangerous—he just couldn't help himself. These examples just show you there is nothing new under the sun.

Similarly, in Joshua 23:12-13 Joshua describes soul ties which would cause the nation to sin. "¹²But if you turn away from him and intermarry with the survivors of these nations remaining among you, ¹³then know for certain that the LORD your God will no longer drive them out from your land. Instead, they will be a snare and a trap to you, a pain in your side and a thorn in your eyes, and you will be wiped out from this good land the LORD your God has given you." There would be a permanent problems and potential for loss by their ungodly connections with the people of the land.

The key to all deliverance is legal grounds. Proverbs 26:2 (KJV) "²As the bird by wandering, as the swallow by flying, so the curse causeless shall not come." As long as an ungodly soul tie exists, whether to an object, person, or sin, the enemy has legal grounds, so the tie needs to be broken, and repented of, and any objects, if relevant, need to be discarded. The enemy needs legal grounds.

Additionally, there may be soul ties to places. Remember Lot's wife. Genesis 19:23 – 26 (NLT) "²³The sun was rising as Lot reached the village. ²⁴Then the LORD rained down fire and burning sulfur from the heavens on Sodom and Gomorrah. ²⁵He utterly destroyed them, along with the other cities and villages of the plain, eliminating all life—people, plants, and animals alike. ²⁶But Lot's wife looked back as she was following along behind him, and she became a pillar of salt." She lost her future because she was tied to her past. It was a place she desired more than what God provided for her and her family. A person can have a soul tie to a bar or a club, a street or a house. Maybe God has told you to move out of a location, but you are so tied to it, and the people you know there, you have a hard time leaving. Seek the Lord on this, ask for His grace, and go.

On the other hand, a good soul tie to a place is described in the relationship between the Jewish people and the Promised Land. The land of Canaan was given to the Jews through the Abrahamic covenant. The Jews were tied by God to the land—it was His land and He decided who would inhabit it. Even though they went through great turmoil and judgment, causing them to be carried away to Babylon and scattered throughout the earth, they came back to the land and continue to do so. The land is, was and always will be their place of occupation because God said so.

Remember, many soul ties, of whatever kind, may be pleasurable, or bring back pleasurable memories, but we have to evaluate them with regard to our growth and the word of God.

Some relationships are mixed. For example, we can have good soul ties to a relative, such as a spouse or parent, but there can be ungodly parts of that relationship—perhaps ungodly manipulation, control, or domination. In such a case, repent of and forgive others for the ungodly elements, and learn to move out in freedom in the relationship. Parents have a strong potential for transference of spirits, idolatry, and control. Any incestuous relationship is out of the will of God and has great potential for harm, whether it was emotionally incestuous or sexually incestuous. Even if a child or family member had no real choice in the matter, and did not sin, ties need to be broken, and hearts healed.

Perhaps a child's growth has been stunted by domination of another person, a parent or older sibling. The child is not allowed to think or feel for themselves or mature because the personality of another, substitutes their judgment, life, thoughts, desires in place of the child's, blocking individual growth, initiative, or even reliance upon God. Such ungodly domination is widespread between parents and children, husbands and wives, even pastors and congregations—and those are what we would consider "normal" relationship patterns. Consider the "boundary-less" world of today. The control imprisons the individual and disables the individual from ever developing the skills and vision to be mature. It also serves to strip the individual of the dignity and skills they do have. Control lasts into adulthood, and leaves emotional marks, and creates a lasting impact even after the death of the dominating person. This is not God's plan at all, God wants us to mature and grow into the image of His Son, not someone else. Godly parents need to facilitate the transference of childhood dependence from themselves, to Father God, weaning the child not only from the parent, but also the things of this earth, from self-interest and self-absorption, so the child is nurtured in Christ, and grows into a child of God. This is the ideal. I don't know how often this happens, but it is the ideal. Luke 2: "[52]And Jesus increased in wisdom and stature, and in favor with God and man." We will deal a little later on with stunted growth. As the domination and control is broken, the true person can grow to full stature.

Like Hannah and her little Samuel, the "little Samuels" of this world truly belong to God. When released by their parents to Him (though not necessarily in the shelter of a physical temple--certainly in the shelter of the Almighty), in the everyday events of life, with the influence of God in their lives, they will be empowered to grow into their divine destinies. This is not about human empowerment or human potential movements; this is about connecting into the plan for each life decided in the councils of heaven before the foundation of the world. This is what God wants.

An individual so exposed to such ungodly dominating influence needs that false spiritual influence and ungodly emotional soul tie broken. The personality, habits, soul, and spirits of the dominating person need to be detached from the individual. The Bible shows us many examples of people knit together in godly ways and those tied in ungodly ways. The ungodly ways must be broken. No one's soul should be connected in such a way with another person that an individual cannot worship God in spirit and in truth, with truth in the inward parts. We should not have to compromise, cringe, or miss God's purpose and destiny for our lives. We are overcomers when every part of us cleansed and quickened by the Holy Spirit. God has His boundaries and design for our personalities.

In ministering freedom, we need to break the power and control of the dominating personality. This may be done in general i.e., "I break all evil power, possession and control of X over Y in Jesus' name," but it is also valuable to be specific. Address specific events, types of activities, places, conversations, areas of life, (for example, clothes, friends, food, choice of a mate, types of abuse, spiritual expression, emotional responses), where unbiblical control was asserted, break the power of "X's" control over "Y" in these circumstances, and release the true life of God into the soul. Human plans and designs of one person over another, no matter how well meaning, can imprison lives. When these shells are broken, the human being can grow out of the seed formed in the natural to the plant intended by the Spirit of God. Also spirits of manipulation and control, Jezebel, witchcraft, and domination of the controller working with passivity, self-hatred, self-rejection and other spirits of victim need to be commanded to leave. Family line sin patterns and curses in such domination, control, passivity and victimization need to be repented of and broken.

Then ask the Holy Spirit to bring His creative, healing work to your soul, so that the power of another person can no longer tug on your adult personality. Just as the waters of the Red Sea covered the Egyptians pursuing the children of Israel who they held in bondage for over 400 years, the past can be covered and washed over. Love covers a multitude of sins. The love of God can so rise up that offenses are cleansed, flooded and unrecognized. When the "Red Sea" of the red blood of Jesus covers the Satanic pursuers of God's children, we can truly say, "I once knew a person who lived in bondage, but he doesn't live there anymore." Therapy and counseling can rearrange the traumas and problems of our lives and give us guidance as to our responses, even help us process losses, traumas, disappointments in time, but only the Son can set us free. "Normal", working (functioning) Christian families, churches, religious groups have ungodly control mechanisms and domination at times, so being raised in a Christian home or attending a church does not avoid control. These are patterns deeply ingrained in the human heart.

In general, breaking ungodly soul ties:

Repent of ungodly dimension of the relationship, repent of sin associated with that relationship. Forgive those who have dominated or controlled you. Break ties to the person, object, smell, memory, or place. Break all evil power, possession, control and authority of that person, place, object, or experience has had in your life. Get rid of paraphernalia, objects, tattoos, even apps on your phone or electronic devices that keep you in bondage. Do it all in Jesus' name.

With regard to soul ties with a person, command any part of the soul of person to leave you and related demons. In Appendix D there are prayers to break ungodly soul ties. I have talked to gang members who don't think they can be set free, and are fearful, and I have ministered to gang members who want to be free and will accept God's offer of freedom and protection. The choice is always ours. God is bigger than any problem we will ever have.

I am going to let you in on a big reality. Freedom is difficult and there is a cost. God desires freedom for the believer, and a life of freedom to follow Him. The world system is not geared towards freedom. Religions, other than Christianity as declared by the scripture, and I am saying this because there is a lot of distortion of the word of God keeping people in bondage, are not geared towards true freedom. Political systems are not geared towards freedom. The world is designed to keep us spiritually immature and under the influence of the prince of the power of the air. "Anything goes" is not free, it is the highway to slavery. There is a cost for freedom, and the road to life is narrow. There is only true freedom in Christ, His boundaries, His holiness and His endless possibilities. The just shall live by faith. Lots of people don't want it or don't want to pay the price for it. Actually Jesus has already paid the price for our deliverance, healing and restoration. But there is a price we pay too. The price we pay is submitting ourselves and humbling ourselves to the process of deliverance and wholeness, just like Naaman. We can only want it by the grace of God. By grace are you saved and continue to be saved through faith, for full holiness and wholeness in Christ, it is a gift of God, lest anyone should boast.

Fifth Level: The Inner Meditations of our Hearts: Attitudes, Vows, Negative Core Beliefs

Fifth Level of Cleansing and Healing: This also works with inner healing in the section following.

On this level the renewing of our mind is required in a whole new dimension. When I say the renewing of our minds, I do not limit this to our mental thought life, such as "what am I thinking now at this minute," or "what are my memories of an event." This does not even match-up with scripture. I am including the emotional patterns developed over the years, the paths of feeling, the memories stored in our bodies, minds, and hearts, inner meditations that are almost unconscious. David cried, "Create in me a new heart, O Lord, and renew a right spirit within me." We are also taken to the Psalms 19:14 which states the "let the words of my mouth and meditations of my heart being acceptable to the Lord." These deep levels need to be renewed by the old ways being dismantled and sanctified and the new ways developed step-by-step with the word of God, and reinforced or renewed by the healing and creative power of the Holy Spirit. The explicit thought life is a very small portion of this. Renewing of the mind does not just mean getting rid of bad patterns or ways of thinking and replacing these with God's truth for our lives, but also, sanctifying that which is good— all by the power of the Holy Spirit. You are the temple of the Holy Spirit. Good and bad and everything in between are to be presented to the Lord.

One of the key scriptures on this is Romans 12: "[1] I beseech you therefore, brethren, by the mercies of God, that ye present your bodies a living sacrifice, holy, acceptable unto God, *which is* your reasonable service. [2] And be not conformed to this world: but be ye transformed by the renewing of your mind, that ye may prove what *is* that good, and acceptable, and perfect, will of God."

An important first step is just to present our bodies as a sacrifice. We lay ourselves on the altar of faith and obedience. Lay your life down. Let the Lord cleanse your heart to make it holy and acceptable to God. Do not be like the world around you, but be transformed by the renewing of your mind, so that our lives can prove by experience and example which is the good, acceptable and perfect will of God. We often want to change the world around us for an external change of our circumstances, but the Lord wants to change us so we can change the world for His purposes. Our demands for inner justice might better be met by forgiveness and release and then proactively allowing God to change us so that changed person can influence others.

We ask, who is our enemy? Some people will say the enemy is this person or that person, some group or political party. While there is a level of truth to that (at times), Jesus never focused on His outside enemies. He could have spent His whole life complaining about the Romans or the Jews. His family rejected Him, and did not accept His claims, so He could have complained about them as well. If He wanted to take out the political enemies of Israel, or religious opposition to Himself, He would have come to rule and reign at that time and could easily have done so, but He didn't. He said and did the opposite. He just moved forward to the cross and the resurrection, knowing that because of His death and resurrection ultimately the kingdoms of this world would become the kingdoms of our God. The salvation of the world was procured for those who believe, and that He would be King of Kings and Lord of Lords. He did tell the truth—the Jews rejected the Messiah that was sent to them. It grieved Him terribly. He wept because of it. His mission, however, was to conquer sin and death and all the power of the enemy, and establish another kind of kingdom in our hearts first and then the world. He wanted the world to be saved, not just ruled. So it was going to take time and the co-laboring of that new creation called the church.

Jesus said the kingdom of heaven is within. Luke 17:21. As long as we identify the wrong enemy, we are going to be fighting the wrong battle. God gives us overcoming power on the inside first. As long as life is someone else's fault, we will be focused on the outside battle and we never dealing with the greater problem on the inside.

God is in the business of restoration, focus on the Lord—He knows how to give back to you what has been taken. Also, God knows how to repay, He says vengeance is mine, and I will repay. He knows how to repay both the guilty and the innocent. Yes, people have wronged us, perhaps our families and people. Yes, there have been terrible tragedies, injustices and abuses. That is not to say we minimize trespasses, *but the solution first and foremost is to forgive others.* Otherwise, our lives will be tied to and identified with tragedy not victory and we will spend the rest of our lives, angry, sad, being triggered with pain. I don't want that. I want freedom, freedom to be and become all that God created me to be, not the enemy's disfiguration and degradation. The Lord enables us to gain victory over the pain we have experienced personally and generationally and use it for a purpose, to liberate and bring healing to others. The world will always be filled with offenses. Life is often a mine field. But we have the armor of God for warfare. Maybe not warfare with bombs and missiles, tanks and submarines, but the power of love and truth and faith and the word through the blood of Jesus.

Romans 12:1-2 in the Message Bible, gives a beautiful elaboration of the King James: "¹So here's what I want you to do, God helping you: Take your everyday, ordinary life—your sleeping, eating, going-to-work, and walking-around life—and place it before God as an offering. Embracing what God does for you is the best thing you can do for him. [Let's experience all that the Lord offers in His redemption.] ²Don't become so well-adjusted to your culture that you fit into it without even thinking. Instead, fix your attention on God. You'll be changed from the inside out. Readily recognize what he wants from you, and quickly respond to it. Unlike the culture around you, always dragging you down to its level of immaturity, God brings the best out of you, develops well-formed maturity in you." The cross of Jesus Christ is not for toleration, accommodation or normalization of who we are or the sin we commit, but for revelation, liberation, transformation, sanctification, and elevation.

Being changed from the inside out is really the only kind of change there is. The rest is rearranging the furniture of our lives. This does not mean we do not strive for a better culture or society, but it is automatically going to be better if we shine for Him and live according to His word. Jesus said, you are the light of the world, just as He is the Light of the World. Just as His kingdom was not of this world, neither is ours. Respond to the will of God. In the process we will develop a well formed maturity. The culture is in a state of immaturity—because it is based on the flesh and the mind and spiritual confusion. Unless we are healed and delivered and cleansed and restored, we will be there with them, even if we have accepted Jesus as our Savior. Then we can live out the good and acceptable and perfect will of God, not through the power of our own strength, but through the grace of God, and the flow of the Holy Spirit in us. We are not legally clenching our teeth to be good, or demanding someone else be good, but we have grown in Christ to be like Him and the fruits of goodness and the contagion of His love follow. He wants us to grow to the fullness of His life. We aren't suppressing the old habits and an old nature, we are possessing a new one. John 8: "[36] If the Son therefore shall make you free, ye shall be free indeed."

Note Ephesians 2:1 "And you *hath he quickened*, who were dead in trespasses and sins; [2] Wherein in time past ye walked according to the course of this world, according to the prince of the power of the air, the spirit that now works in the children of disobedience: [3]Among whom also we all had our conversation in times past in the lusts of our flesh, <u>fulfilling the desires of the flesh and of the mind;</u> and were by nature the children of wrath, even as others." We used to try to fulfill the desires of the flesh and of the mind, our emotional and social lives were in the environment of the lusts of the flesh, we were under the power of the spirit that works in the children of disobedience, but now we are not.

Philippians 2: "[5] Let this mind be in you which was also in Christ Jesus"—what was that? The rest of that scripture describes the mind in Christ Jesus—" [6]Who, being in the form of God, thought it not robbery to be equal with God: [7]But made himself of no reputation, <u>and took upon him the form of a servant,</u> and was made in the likeness of men: [8]And being found in fashion as a man, he humbled himself, and became obedient unto death, even the death of the cross." He took the form of a servant. He humbled Himself and became obedient unto death. No one can do that without the mind of Christ and Christ changing one's mind.

First Corinthians 2:16 "[16] For who hath known the mind of the Lord, that he may instruct him? But we have the mind of Christ." We were once going the opposite direction to the lovely, graceful ways of God: Colossians 1: "[21] And you, that were sometime alienated and enemies in *your* mind by wicked works, yet now hath he reconciled [22] In the body of his flesh through death, to present you holy and unblameable and unreproveable in his sight: [23] If ye continue in the faith grounded and settled, and *be* not moved away from the hope of the gospel, which ye have heard, *and* which was preached to every creature which is under heaven; whereof I Paul am made a minister; [24] Who now rejoice in my sufferings for you, and fill up that which is behind of the afflictions of Christ in my flesh for his body's sake, which is the church."

Ephesians 4: "[20] But ye have not so learned Christ; [21] If so be that ye have heard him, and have been taught by him, as the truth is in Jesus: [22] That ye put off concerning the former conversation the old man, which is corrupt according to the deceitful lusts; [23] And be renewed in the spirit of your mind; [24] And that ye put on the new man, which after God is created in righteousness and true holiness." Put off the old man, be renewed in the spirit of your mind, and put on the new man. Something is formed in us in Christ, the new man, created in righteousness and true holiness.

Finally, Mark 12:30 "[28] And one of the scribes came, and having heard them reasoning together, and perceiving that he had answered them well, asked him, Which is the first commandment of all? [29] And Jesus answered him, The first of all the commandments *is*, Hear, O Israel; The Lord our God is one Lord: [30] And thou shalt love the Lord thy God with all thy heart, and with all thy soul, and with all thy mind, and with all thy strength: this *is* the first commandment. [31] And the second *is* like, *namely* this, Thou shalt love thy neighbour as thyself. There is none other commandment greater than these." I conclude by saying that we cannot love the Lord with all our mind, heart, soul and strength until He is Lord over all. This requires the step-by-step yielding of our intents, motives, emotions, thoughts, pain, damages, lusts and desires to Him on a daily basis, unfolding the past layer by layer. We cannot love our neighbors without loving ourselves, and we cannot love ourselves until that love is birthed in truth by the Spirit and Word of God. We cannot love ourselves without determining the boundaries of obedience and the limitless experience of God's true love, and find our true identity in Him, which is a work of the cross and resurrection in us. Loving our neighbors is operating in obedience to the scripture and the Spirit of God in relationship to others.

Therefore, what are some of the steps we can take for the renewing of our minds? The preceding pages of this book are all patterns of renewal, but I suggest some more:

1. Identifying sources of shame, grief, abandonment, neglect, trauma, and more, and undoing the works of the devil step-by-step through the power of the Holy Spirit and knowing and integrating into our being what the word of God says about our lives. What did we experience and how did that distort our image of ourselves, God and others? What were the dynamics of our family of origin? Was there control, addiction or abuse issues, for example? What were your parent's patterns of failure or disappointment? What were the life altering experiences we had and which our families had? We must identify the attitudes in our hearts, our understanding, our beliefs about people and ourselves so we can replace the painful with the gainful. We cannot deny what has happened, we must face truth. Truth is the liberator with the power of the Holy Spirit, under the direction of the Holy Spirit and the love of the Father and the Son. But remember the "truth" of God, while not denying the truth of our history and experiences, transcends them, and it is this transcendent experience that elevates us and overrides and sanctifies what we have experienced. <u>A lot of this is going to interface with the other levels of deliverance and healing I have outlined.</u>

We are perfectly formed in Him from creation by salvation to carry the image of Christ. I believe we discover this as we process the reasons and results of our separation from Him, ourselves and others. When God created man and woman and all of creation, He said it was "very good." God's design for human body, soul and spirit was a "very good" creation. After the fall, Satan, sin and death "de-formed," "dis-informed," and "un-formed" all of this. In one sense when we are restored internally by the Lord, <u>we hearken back to the goodness of God's original creation</u>—it is our pattern for identity and living, and then we hearken forward to Christ, because we are as He is in the world and now created in His image. We understand what we were designed to be, and that was initially good. But this process is made real by the Spirit of God, and perfection in Christ. We are made perfect in Christ. <u>Christ</u> is who we are becoming and carrying in our mortal bodies. We were created in the image of God, uncreated by sin, but then recreated in the image of Christ Jesus by the cross and resurrection.

    2. Another important step is grieving our losses. Isaiah 53:4 says "Surely He has borne our griefs and carried our sorrows." Instead of placing barriers against feeling those losses and sorrows, or raising the arguments of denial, we must identify what these losses are, how they originated, the part other people played in our grief and sorrow and our part. By the power and illumination of the Holy Spirit working in the Spirit's timing and strategy we identify the barriers and defense mechanisms we established to protect our hearts—see below. We must repent, submit the patterns to the Lord, break down the defenses, reject denial, and do all the spiritual groundwork needed to just grieve and feel. So much of our emotional illness and mental distress is based on the suppression of grief rather than the expression of it. This also relates to identifying pain and experiencing it with the Holy Spirit this time. It allows the Holy Spirit to enter traumas that may have frozen us in the past. In the process, repent and forgive, be delivered and healed. He has carried and buried our griefs and sorrows, so we need not bury them our hearts. He carried and buried them at His cross, death, and the resurrection. All of this is not an immediate process. The Lord has timing based on His sovereign plans in our lives, and timing as to when we can receive healing. Nevertheless, the Holy Spirit can do more in a second, than other methods can do in a lifetime.

    Pain is a thief, and the thief comes to steal kill and destroy. When much of our lives is stolen by pain, we do not move out in opportunities God presents. Because of pain, our eyes are blinded; because of pain we hurt and hate and have anger. Pain must be nursed and taken care of, and that takes a lot of energy. But when inner sickness is gone, the pain leaves too. In much of our lives we make ourselves sicker by trying to resolve pain in our own ways. Usually this is by the path of least resistance to deal with the problems, rather than go to the root. We seek out a relationship, a drug, distraction, anything but going to the Lord. Finally, the Lord mercifully brings His peace to our hearts—peace by the blood of the cross and peace through the Holy Spirit's indwelling presence. Many people have experienced terrible losses and tragedies. The Bible says that there is a time to mourn. That is important, but the Bible also says He carried our griefs, and so, in some way, with God's help, He gives us the strength and power to move on with the living.

3. Identifying defense mechanisms and allowing the Lord to dismantle them. Such mechanisms may be, among others, denial (refusal to believe the truth or pretending it isn't so painful, convicting, destructive), acting out (acting out suppressed or denied emotions in anger or improper actions), rationalization (it wasn't so bad, or I understand how they were this way), or detachment (just shutting off when pain or conflict or something unpleasant comes up), transference or projection of our issues to someone else (the problem is the other person, not me), self-rejection, disqualification of self from relationships to avoid pain, anger. There are many ways we protect ourselves. The help of a good or godly therapist or anointed minister can help identify what we are doing to avoid pain, conflict, or anxiety, and then could facilitate taking down our defensive reactions so we can authentically relate to life in a godly manner. These spiritual and emotional transactions take a while. Our defenses are hidden even to ourselves. Even if you don't go to a therapist the Holy Spirit can show you, "you know, every time I talk to my sister/brother/cousin/parent/spouse, I get defensive and shut down or become another person." Repent, and ask for God's help and go to the root. The Lord told Abraham that He was his exceedingly great shield and reward. Genesis 15:1 (NKJV) "¹After these things the word of the LORD came to Abram in a vision, saying, "Do not be afraid, Abram. I *am* your shield, your exceedingly great reward." Abraham didn't have to defend himself, the Lord did that. Unfortunately, as we grow up, we spend a lot of time defending ourselves, which then takes on a life in its own, perhaps leading to a false self. This comes down to healing, and then trusting the Lord—a lifelong journey.

4. Identifying false selves. In a way this is impersonating our own lives. When dismantled, we can let the true person come forth in faith to Christ. It also comes back to defense mechanisms, adaptations in our childhood, responses to trauma, peer pressure and many other sources. In some ways, this is the state of the human race. We are not truly who we are unless we are born again in Christ and growing into His image. No matter how authentic a person may be, we were created to be that authentic person with a divine dimension in Christ. It is true that some people are mentally and emotionally healthier than others, but our true nature (engaging body, soul <u>and</u> spirit) is expressed in and through Christ. He lives in us and we live in Him.

5. Going to the issue of who is the true person? Was that person allowed to live in the home in which you grew up? Was that person put in a corner, marginalized, suppressed? Did that person commit emotional suicide—just cutting off feelings or numbing them with drugs or alcohol, for example? Are we comfortable in letting the real person exist without the protective layers? So with the Lord we can be born again, and obtain who we really are through His love and healing. Psalms 139 tells us that He created each part, and we are wonderfully and fearfully made, that we have destiny and a divine design before the foundation of the world. The challenge before us is to receive the healing, deliverance and restoration God offers so that we can move into that destiny.

6. Core beliefs—are our core beliefs negative such as nothing ever works out for me, no matter how hard I try I just can't get ahead, or everyone leaves me, or I am damaged goods, bad, shameful, guilty, ugly, life is painful, I cannot get close to people, etc.? Core beliefs are hard to break and they can only be changed by processing the bad, and acknowledging the good, that God created, and destined for our lives. Our old nature is very accustomed and even comfortable with the negative. It is a work of the Holy Spirit to <u>override, process, and erase</u> these core beliefs with the new nature, which we must follow daily—putting on the new man. The inner ability of our hearts to have faith about life and ourselves is not an overnight process. It requires sifting, dying to self, acting in faith, obedience, exposure to the word, healing, revelation of who we truly are, among other experiences. Our souls and spirits will come to life experiencing Christ in us every day. No one has big faith about their life, the world, or others, in a minute. We all have a measure of faith, yet application of this in the daily experiences of life and our negative core beliefs is a learning process. Start with the faith that is the size of a mustard seed. Remember we have the great Holy Spirit as the Helper. He is going to uplift us even if we don't feel like being uplifted at times.

7. When we are broken and lost we not only curse ourselves, but make vows which stop the flow of God's love and provision in life. For example, a child or adult may vow never to trust anyone again after being hurt by a loved one. This vow may be on a subconscious level. A man may vow to retaliate after being overwhelmed by a competitor. A woman vows to make all men pay for the hurt she has received and never trust again. We can make vows of silence. Sometimes parents force their children to make ungodly promises. Vows of obligation, vows of dedication, vows regarding the direction of one's life that are out of the will of God, need to be broken in the name of Jesus. This provides release so the true activities of God can occur. Demonic support of these vows need to be broken. Vows under false religions, dedication to their deities, dedications to demonic entities, to organizations, and more, need to be broken. The wounds or traumas behind the vows require the healing of the Holy Spirit. Then the rubble will be cleared away so the individual can walk a clear straight path, and godly defenses built with the armor of God. The shield of faith, breastplate of righteousness, helmet of salvation, sword of the Spirit, feet shod with the preparation of the gospel of peace, loins girt with truth, are more than sufficient to protect our lives.

Sixth Level: Healing of the Heart. Deprivation, Loss, Legitimate Needs that are Unmet

I should call this "Fast Forward." God heals us and grows us up.

1. Jesus came to heal the broken hearted, and He does just that. Luke 4: [18] The Spirit of the Lord is upon me, because he hath anointed me to preach the gospel to the poor; he hath sent me to heal the brokenhearted, to preach deliverance to the captives, and recovering of sight to the blind, to set at liberty them that are bruised." Like an urgent mission from heaven, the Spirit of Lord was upon Jesus to heal the brokenhearted. This was a vital mission from the Father, because broken hearts mean fractured and crippled lives. God was tired of His loved ones being unable to love Him, love themselves, and love each other. He ached at their grief, knowing that their grief made them weak and the brokenness made it impossible for them to function in a godly manner. He wanted to be loved by His creation and He wanted His creation to exist in an atmosphere of love, so He needed to heal us first. Only the Lord Jesus, only the Holy Spirit, only the Father can heal broken hearts. If hearts do not get healed, they become hard and distracted, and leave the paths of life. So the Father sent Jesus on a vital mission with the power of the Holy Spirit to go into any heart that would permit Him to be there. The Father said, once you are there, release My healing. Follow all the trails of pain and confusion up and down the corridors of these hearts and trust in My creative power to put the pieces back together again, restore the crippled ones back to wholeness. Heal them even before they understand what is happening to them, for if they are healed and forgiven they will automatically love Me and rise up in faith to serve Me.

Jesus said the Spirit of the Lord is upon Me. Not just any "me" and not just any spirit. He was a willing vessel to take the message of love, and live it, and deliver the goods to the home and heart of you and me. Somebody had to deliver the goods. That person had to be willing to love and be hurt—sometimes ministry is like that. Jesus had to live the love to give the love. God is love. He had to know how to deliver the package of love to the right address, at the right time and the right way. The wisdom of the Father determined it, the love of the Son performed it, and the power of the Holy Spirit enabled it. The Holy Spirit is the One Who destroys the yoke.

To everyone who is reading this right now, Jesus has the right key for the day, month, year your life fell apart, the right key for the day you were hurt by your spouse, parent, friend, the key for the little boy and girl trapped in insecurity waiting for the approval of an absent father or disinterested mother, the key to the neglect and abuse you experienced as a child, the key to the day you started in the wrong path, and anything else you have experienced. He has the key for our immaturity, and the key to advance us to further glory. For some people He has the key to release them to the appropriate identity. He has the key to release the gifts and talents that have been locked up for decades, and all of you have them. He has the key to unlock your future and destiny and divine inheritance. Will you let Jesus into the rooms of your heart and then take those keys He has shown you, and set others free? We have the keys to the kingdom and He has the key of David, to open doors that no man can shut and shut doors that no man can open. I think with a combination of these keys, the word of God, the blood of Jesus and the power of the Holy Spirit, much can be accomplished in the human soul and personal destiny.

The same healing power that is releases lame people from lameness, cleanses lepers from leprosy, heals blind people from blindness, comes into our hearts and binds our wounds, to release sad people from sadness. When I minister inner healing to people, I pray that the healing power of God will go into the wounds and restore the soul. Deliverance and healing must be ministered together. You can get set free, but what about the wounds that cry out? If that wound is still there, the possibility of infection still exists. The blood of Abel who was betrayed and murdered by his brother cries out—representing the injustice and betrayal we all experience especially by those closest to us, but the blood of Jesus is of a far higher frequency and power, and that blood takes us to a higher level of experience, a God level. Hebrews 11: "[24]And to Jesus the mediator of the new covenant, and to the blood of sprinkling, that speaketh better things than *that of* Abel." <u>God forgives the offender and heals the wounded.</u> Our hearts carry many injustices from childhood and beyond. The cross evens the score and brings healing to the wounds. The cross is for the wounded and the abuser, the victim and victimizer, the good and the bad, the right and the wrong.

We all know the story of the good Samaritan. Luke 10: "[30]And Jesus answering said, A certain man went down from Jerusalem to Jericho, and fell among thieves, which stripped him of his raiment, and wounded him, and departed, leaving him half dead. [31]And by chance there came down a certain priest that way: and when he saw him, he passed by on the other side. [32]And likewise a Levite, when he was at the place, came and looked on him, and passed by on the other side. [33]But a certain Samaritan, as he journeyed, came where he was: and when he saw him, he had compassion on him, [34]And went to him, and bound up his wounds, pouring in oil and wine, and set him on his own beast, and brought him to an inn, and took care of him. [35]And on the morrow when he departed, he took out two pence, and gave them to the host, and said unto him, Take care of him; and whatsoever thou spendest more, when I come again, I will repay thee."

Let's take a look first at the man at the side of the road. He started on a journey from Jerusalem to Jericho, and got beat up. There, broken and bleeding on the ground, he couldn't move or help himself. Life is like that. We start on a journey, but at some point thieves (and the master thief, Satan) overpower us, and we are broken and bleeding unable to get up and finish our journey. Sometimes this violation comes from the outside, without our consent, and sometimes it comes through our own bad choices—as has been described in multiple ways in this book. Perhaps we have ignorantly started a journey alone, and should have gotten help. The thief beats us up, strips us of our dignity, and leaves us at the side of the road for dead. The religious people avoided the man. Religion never healed anyone. Religion doesn't have the power to save. It may have a form of godliness and even do good, but it does not have the anointing for wholeness and salvation. Jesus went about "doing good" AND "healing all those oppressed of the devil."

But let's focus on the man who came to help. Thankfully, the Lord God picks us up through His servants. The Samaritan was an outcast man himself—rejected by the Jews (like Jesus), but he ministers the oil and the wine to the beaten man. The wine represents the cleansing blood of Jesus, which has the power to forgive sins, break soul ties, set us free from demons, and more. The oil represents the Holy Spirit, which brings healing and new life. That is how wounds are healed, they are cleansed through repentance and forgiveness, taking out the infection, demons, and other areas needing deliverance, all that the blood can do, and then the power of God comes in and brings healing, like the flow of oil. Next, the wound is bound up. The broken man needs a period for rest and restoration. We cannot proceed with full activity when we are in the healing process. He has to be carried to that place of rest as well. Not only is the violation washed away, but the breach is healed, and he is given time for his body to be restored. The man will still remember he was beat up, but the wound will be gone. A potential nightmare is turned around to be an experience of God's love that speaks for the ages.

No one with a broken leg can run a race in the natural. Jesus knew that people with broken hearts could not run the race of faith and life. When we pray for deliverance, we need to pray for healing too. That was Jesus' inaugural sermon to people in a synagogue, in other words, an established place of worship under the old covenant. Likewise, there are lot of hurting people in the church. Just accepting Jesus as our Savior doesn't resolve the hurts and conflicts of our lives—but it does give us new start to a life in Christ. God wants to put us on our feet to run the race of faith now. Our initial trust in Jesus Christ is the first step in growth.

2. Secondly, there is another dimension of restoration. Note, this is "restoration," not healing. That is the area of legitimate developmental needs that are not met. These are not areas of emotional damage, sin, or demonic oppression. They are just gaps in growth which

parents, caretakers, or others have not activated or enabled, through their ignorance, disinterest, abandonment, lack of nurture, lack of understanding, the busyness of life and work, personal sickness, absence, whatever reason. That doesn't mean they didn't love the child, but perhaps they didn't have a clue about God's will for the child (you), things just fell through the cracks, lack of understanding, or it was just the result of the sin nature in all of us. Parents/ caretakers are supposed to "call out" a child and help them form their identity consistent with scripture. A lot of damage can occur from these gaps—resulting in sin, demons, brokenness, but the damage and results are not the same as the gaps. Natural parents are supposed to help children mature and grow. Each parent has a part, though due to a multiplicity of reasons it often doesn't happen. That doesn't mean they are bad people. Even the best of homes, Christian homes, fall short to some degree, because in the end, there are areas of growth that can only be activated by God the Father by intimacy with Him, because we are all born into a fallen world. Finally, no one in the natural can ultimately raise us to the stature of Christ.

Part of this is identifying unmet needs in our lives—lack of nurture, neglect, lack of attachment, and why these needs were not met. Then we go to the Lord with the pain and emptiness, asking Him to fill the gaps. We also may need to repent for our own part in keeping our lives stunted—perhaps our own stubbornness, willfulness, defensiveness and pride. The subsequent result is that God can restore the growth that did not occur at the appropriate time, because He can restore the years that locust and cankerworm have eaten away. Joel 2:20. I believe the Lord can "jumpstart" us as we identify our losses and lack of growth through the power of the Holy Spirit. Except that this time the growth will be under the parenting of the Father, the power of the Holy Spirit and through Jesus Christ, and sanctified in a new dimension. Again, the Lord restores the years that the locust and cankerworm have eaten away, not just in material goods like a home or a car or what you should have had or was taken away, but the person you should have been—God's design, God's identity, God's purpose, God's image. He is the Resurrection and the Life. Prayer in this area is to enable growth of the one-year old, two-year old, five-year old, ten-year old. We may also pray for the true identity to come forth. Who is the real person—come alive. Who is the real boy or girl—come alive! God can do things quicker than natural means. Jesus called the little girl to come back to life –"little girl arise"– in Mark chapter 5:41. Today Jesus calls the little boy or girl in us to come to life, in the emotional realm as well. Some people have hardly even met this little boy or girl. How to pray for this? Pray for the child at age 1 or 2, 3 or 4, 5 or 6, or whatever, to mature and develop as God intended. Call that child forth to break through the walls of limitation or brokenness or pain or whatever the Holy Spirit shows you. Pray that growth of the true person would be "jumpstarted." Pray that the person "now" would embrace the person "then" and experience who they are.

In a bigger dimension, Christ is bringing us to a maturity in love, and this is a lifelong process. Ephesians 4: "[11]And he gave some, apostles; and some, prophets; and some, evangelists; and some, pastors and teachers; [12] For the perfecting of the saints, for the work of the ministry, for the edifying of the body of Christ: [13] <u>Till we all come in the unity of the faith, and of the knowledge of the Son of God, unto a perfect man, unto the measure of the stature of the fullness of Christ:</u> [14] That we henceforth be no more children, tossed to and fro, and carried about with every wind of doctrine, by the sleight of men, and cunning craftiness, whereby they lie in wait to deceive; [15] But speaking the truth in love, may grow up into him in all things, which is the head, even Christ:". We are always going to be growing into a divine life, a supernatural life which is bigger than the definitions and boundaries of our natural lives. God stretches us and helps us grow into maturity in Christ. This is different from emotional gaps and lack of development. <u>Our lives are bigger than our lives.</u> The maturity of Christ's love operating in us is going to challenge every single one of us, all the days of our lives—breaking down the small house of our lives to dwell in the bigger house of God's plan and purpose—a God-centered life instead of a self-centered life. Jesus has prepared a place for us in His Father's house. I believe that is not only for our final destination, but here as well. Only Jesus loves to the uttermost, that is why He can save to the uttermost. But in some dimension, all of us are called to a divine love, to fulfill something of the ministry of Christ on this earth, in the bigness of Jesus Christ.

3. Attachment needs i.e. meeting attachment needs through our relationship with God, godly relationships, and healing. The Bible tells us that when father or mother forsake us, the Lord is there. Psalms 27:10. Our attachment to loving parents, for example, help us grow and thrive and mature. The mutual love, including the nurture and direction of parents, and the innocent dependency of the child, form a bond that helps the child become who God created them to be and produces joy between the parties. The trauma of attachment loss or deprivation is a deep one that must be repaired layer by layer. These attachment losses can be met by the Lord as we yield our hearts to Him, and they can be restored in godly relationships and prayer. The growth of the inner person that is enabled by attachment needs being met can be realized even when one is no longer a child, enabling also the development of an identity that perhaps was never formed, but now is formed in Christ. This is supernatural growth.

Many believers grow older with legitimate attachment needs that are not met. If these are not met, we cannot grow and become what God has created us to be. There is nothing to be ashamed of if you have experienced neglect, abuse, or abandonment—we all need that bonding with our parents, especially with a same sex parent or good substitute. Someone needs to help us grow into adulthood. The absence of such emotional connections and the absence of mature formative input from parents creates a huge hole in a person's heart. There are many spiritual orphans out there. People have written volumes on attachment needs, trauma to identity, gender, mother wounds and father wounds, when there is an absence of love between parent and child. (See Appendix G and H for Understanding and Healing the Mother Wound/Father Wound, repectively.) But again, the power of the Holy Spirit can "fast forward" our broken hearts so we can connect with ourselves and others in a mature and joyful way, as we forgive and submit our brokenness to the Lord. In this broken society and broken world, cravings send us searching for attachment where we can find it. Sometimes we find a series of sinful attachments, like the woman at the well in John chapter 4; but by grace, we find God, like the woman at the well in John chapter 4. The church is meant to be a place where brothers and sisters and spiritual mothers and fathers can help repair the breaches. Belonging is built into us. The Lord puts us in the body of Christ and godly relationships. You need others and others need you.

We often fix ourselves outside of the boundaries of God, when these legitimate needs and pains are not addressed. God knows our losses—but He also knows our gains, and how we can be restored in the areas of deprivation and wasted years. Again, He will restore the years that the locust and cankerworm have eaten away—whether these were our fault or not. The newness of Christ can flourish in us, as the gaps are restored and the connections that were needed are supplied by His grace. The Lord desires truth in the inward parts. This is the key, as our hearts submit in truth to the Lord, He pours into us the larger Truth of Himself and His design and plans for us are revealed, and true liberation can occur. As the smaller life yields to the larger life and vision, we become sons and daughters of God.

SEVENTH LEVEL: DYING TO SELF, AND THEN, WALKING IN NEWNESS OF LIFE

The Seventh Level of Restoration:

Every believer lives in the dynamic of the cross and the resurrection. We take up our crosses daily and follow Jesus. It is the dynamic of the new resurrection life, leaving the old ways of thinking and feeling behind, and being led of the Holy Spirit and empowered by the Holy Spirit to live as sons and daughters of God in our new life in Christ. Dying to the old life and living to the new is not a dreadful march, a forced march or a death march, but entering into a greater and divine dimension of life. We release an old life to enter into a new life.

First the dying process. Through the cross of Jesus Christ, we die and then we live. While in the case of deliverance or healing there is a definite end to some issues in our lives, dying to the flesh is ongoing and won't end until we transition to heaven. It also is closely aligned with being a living sacrifice. We die to the flesh and the false life. We live to God. As stated earlier, we put off the old man and take on the new man. But only then can the great God life come out of the frail self life. John 12:23 - 28 (NLT) "²³Jesus replied, "The time has come for the Son of Man to enter into his glory. ²⁴The truth is, a kernel of wheat must be planted in the soil. Unless it dies it will be alone—a single seed. But its death will produce many new kernels—a plentiful harvest of new lives. ²⁵Those who love their life in this world will lose it. Those who despise their life in this world will keep it for eternal life. ²⁶All those who want to be my disciples must come and follow me, because my servants must be where I am. And if they follow me, the Father will honor them. ²⁷Now my soul is deeply troubled. Should I pray, 'Father, save me from what lies ahead'? But that is the very reason why I came! ²⁸Father, bring glory to your name." Then a voice spoke from heaven, saying, "I have already brought it glory, and I will do it again."

A seed dies in the ground, but explodes to new life. This is the pattern of our spiritual life. We are like that seed. The seed is initially planted and covered with dirt, and there seems no way out. The seed has no choice as to where it was planted. It is dark and confining for the seed. Add to that, heat and moisture, and the seed feels like it is going to explode. Then one day it does explode, but the explosion, while causing death to the seed in its original unattractive form, a form that only contains potential, launches it to a new glorious dimension of life that was locked in the seed. That is our life in Christ.

I consider dying to self a bit like falling on the Rock of Jesus. We struggle, we fall on Him, we humble ourselves, we seek His way, we obey, and then He enables us to go forward. We die to our own ways of living and doing things, and live to God's commands and ways. We yield to His grace and the word of God. We let Him break and change us into His image. I like these words from Psalms 5 in the Message Bible: Psalms 5:3 (TMSG) "³Every morning you'll hear me at it again. <u>Every morning I lay out the pieces of my life on your altar and watch for fire to descend</u>." Yet in that yielding and dying process we learn to walk with Him. Matthew 11:29-30 (TMSG) "²⁹Walk with me and work with me—watch how I do it. <u>Learn the unforced rhythms of grace. I won't lay anything heavy or ill-fitting on you.</u> ³⁰Keep company with me and you'll learn to live freely and lightly." Walking with Jesus teaches us to learn the unforced rhythms of grace. Bow down and yield and live in the flow of God's grace. The struggle with the flesh is hard, but the rewards are infinite.

Sometimes there is dying to self comes in the form of persecution, martyrdom, dreams that die, expectations that are radically changed. We do not understand, and yet there is a bigger God out there than we can imagine and so we trust Him with our lives and hearts. God must give us grace for all of this because it is beyond our natural understanding.

Jesus learned obedience through the things He suffered. Jesus could have run from the cross. Surely He was tempted to run. He sweat drops of blood in anticipation of bearing the sins of the world and suffering humiliation and pain. But His statement in the Garden of Gethsemane saved the world, "Not My will but Thine be done."

You can forget the entire Bible if Jesus had not said and lived these seven words. All of salvation hinges on His surrender to the will of the Father. The cross is not our enemy, but our tree of life. The cross was His destiny and the destiny of all who follow Him. The scripture tells us that what was foolishness to the world was the power of God. Embrace the cross. At the cross "sons of men" die, stale kingdoms are toppled, and unnatural orders based in sin reversed, so that new men and women may be born again and made alive in Jesus Christ the Risen King. God chooses the cross for all His sons and daughters and they must choose it as well—there is no denial and no escape. All roads lead to the cross. Paul writes that for me to live is Christ and to die is gain. Philippians 1:21. Yes, we have our own bodies, but we are His body too and as He is, so are we in the world. I John 4:17. Galatians 2: "[20] I am crucified with Christ: nevertheless I live; yet not I, but Christ liveth in me: and the life which I now live in the flesh I live by the faith of the Son of God, who loved me, and gave himself for me."

Romans 8: "[1] There is therefore now no condemnation to them which are in Christ Jesus, who walk not after the flesh, but after the Spirit. [2] For the law of the Spirit of life in Christ Jesus hath made me free from the law of sin and death." Walking in the law of the Spirit of life in Christ Jesus is the highest way of life. We are a heavenly people, not an earthly people. We are a chosen generation, a royal priesthood. We are not called to live "down" but to live "up." Our eyes are heavenward. Our walk is heavenward. We are seated in heavenly places. Only by the power of God are we able to do this.

But then there is the Living Process. Put on the new man. Ephesians 4: "[24]And that ye put on the new man, which after God is created in righteousness and true holiness."

This is the ultimate in restoration, because we are coming back to the original design that God intended, becoming like the Son of God, but by way of the cross. If sin had not entered the world, Adam and his offspring would have lived and grown in the expansive harmony and glory of divine design and destiny without interruption, being created in the image of God. But since sin did enter the world, we gain this by way of the cross. It is a tough and hard road, and we see through a glass darkly at times, and sometimes that glass is shattered, but the result is glorious. ALL LIFE ALL THE TIME. The shed blood of Jesus interrupts sin and death, and the defective and tragic trajectory ending in death and hell which started in the Garden of Eden, the most perfect of all human environments.

The spiritual themes of this world are redemption, reconciliation, and restoration, as far as God is concerned. But this is the path to heaven, not paradise. John 1: "[12]But as many as received him, to them gave He power to become the sons of God, *even* to them that believe on his name:". To as many as receive Him—that's the starting point. Our creation and salvation merge in Christ. The self-centered life is replaced with the God centered life. We are redeemed by His blood, reconciled to the Father and others, and are restored to the image He desired from the foundation of the world in Jesus Christ and the promises of heaven. Romans 6 is our pattern: "[3]Know ye not, that so many of us as were baptized into Jesus Christ were baptized into his death? [4]Therefore we are buried with him by baptism into death: that like as Christ was raised up from the dead by the glory of the Father, even so we also should walk in newness of life. [5] For if we have been planted together in the likeness of his death, we shall be also in the likeness of his resurrection: [6] Knowing this, that our old man is crucified with him, that the body of sin might be destroyed, that henceforth we should not serve sin. [7] For he that is dead is freed from sin. [8] Now if we be dead with Christ, we believe that we shall also live with him:". We enter into His death to enter into His life, and that is the highest life there is, the intended life in the beginning of creation, and purchased at the cross, with the added dimension of understanding and restoration. We are buried with Him in baptism—we identify with His death. But when we emerge from the water, we are symbolically discarding the grave clothes of an old life, an old identity, and starting a new one—that is our resurrection. Likewise, in deliverance and healing, the grave clothes of an old life are being removed like Lazarus, so we can start over again.

Seven levels of healing, deliverance and restoration. Seven levels of deliverance from the old world and the old ways, healing and strengthening of our hearts, and restoration to the new life of Christ in us. Seven is the number of divine perfection. Seven is God's number and we are in Him and He is in us. We are perfected in Christ, in creation and salvation. Philippians 1: "[6] being confident of this very thing, that He who has begun a good work in you will complete *it* until the day of Jesus Christ." God is bringing His holiness and wholeness to completion in our lives. Psalms 138:8 says God will perfect that which concerns us. Isaiah 60:1 (NKJV) "[1] Arise, shine; For your light has come! And the glory of the LORD is risen upon you." Yes, gross darkness may be in the land, but you are shining with the Son, no longer abandoned at the side of the road, but rising and shining.

Let's go back to the beginning of this book again with the story of Naaman. Naaman, whose body was ravaged by leprosy, dips seven times in the Jordan River at the instruction of the prophet Elisha, and His flesh becomes like that of a newborn baby. Later in the chapter we see that Naaman now believes that the only true God is the God of Israel. He realizes that there is no competition with any God that can heal a person of leprosy. Now let's look at our journey. In this journey of the cross and resurrection presented in this book for deliverance, healing and restoration, I believe that God takes us back to the beginning to start life over with Him by the new birth. He then redeems step-by-step that which has been broken, misdirected, and sinful in us, delivers us from all the power of the enemy, and heals that which has been wounded, as we are reconciled with the Father through Jesus Christ. Finally, He restores our souls and identity in Him, which was His original plan. When He restores our souls we can walk in the paths of righteousness. Our spirits are seated together with Christ in heavenly places, but our souls and bodies must make this heavenward journey. To that end our minds must be renewed and our flesh dies daily until the ultimate resurrection. As I stated earlier, we become born again (like a newborn babe), as Christ is birthed in us, but from the end to the beginning and then back to the end. The process of deliverance, healing and restoration, allows Christ to grow in us, merged into our lives. Life becomes sanctified and He is glorified in us. We are living in Christ and Christ is living in us. As we become sanctified (made holy) and made whole, there will be no doubt that there is no God like our God, Who can reach inside our hearts and make us new.

Next let's consider the man at the pool of Bethesda, described in John chapter 5. Like everyone there, he had been waiting for the moving of the water because once a year something supernatural happened (an angel troubled the waters), and the first one who got into the water was healed. While this looks like a potential miracle to somebody, instead it was a mocking mirage to most everybody. The blind man couldn't see the moving of the water, the lame man, couldn't walk to the water, the sick man was too weak to get there, the tired man was asleep when the angel came, and nobody had help all the time. This man had been there for 38 years. I think the pool of Bethesda in reality was a dumping ground for the sick and infirm—how many friends and family members were going to wait around all day for the unpredictable moving of the waters, everyone lying in their own mess.

But then Jesus went to the pool of Bethesda instead of the feast in Jerusalem. He saw this man and knew he had been there a long time. He asks him the real question—beyond the moving of the waters, beyond the visitation of the angel, beyond all the circumstances, "Do you want to be made whole," because as I said in the beginning of this book, stagnation becomes a way of life. The abnormal becomes normal. Our man at the pool of Bethesda gives a reasonable excuse why he has not gotten into the water—there was no man there to help him and when he tried someone else got there first. We might ponder as well how many of our lives lacked help at important times, when we slipped through the cracks, when we were overlooked, when we were alone. But Jesus' question supersedes the excuses and the reasons and the years of pain—do you want to be made whole? Jesus is here to make us whole if we want it. Jesus gives the command—rise up and walk, and so he does. Get out of there, walk away from it. Take your stuff and leave. You may have known some of these people for 38 years, but they are not going with you, and you don't want to stay with them. Don't look back or leave anything behind. Sometimes we just have to keep walking too. Later Jesus tells him, go and sin no more lest something worse comes upon you, because sin always takes us down, not up, and opens the door to destruction. If we don't have faith in the acts of obedience, we will soon lose faith in other areas of our lives.

The command of Jesus today is to rise up, and keep walking. The healing, delivering, restoring power of God is here to help us to supernatural victory. If you read the story you know only one person at the pool of Bethesda got healed that day, even though the Son of God was there. He was the only one who made it out. Why didn't the others cry for help when they saw this man get healed, rise up and walk? I don't know. The fact of the matter is, not everyone will.

I love Psalms 116. It is considered a Passover psalm and was likely sung or recited by Jesus at the Last Supper. The man in that Psalm had deep troubles, but he called upon the Lord and the Lord heard his cry. The Psalmist writes: "³The sorrows of death compassed me, and the pains of hell gat hold upon me: I found trouble and sorrow. ⁴ Then called I upon the name of the LORD; O LORD, I beseech thee, deliver my soul. ⁵ Gracious is the LORD, and righteous; yea, our God is merciful. ⁶ The LORD preserveth the simple: I was brought low, and he helped me. ⁷ Return unto thy rest, O my soul; for the LORD hath dealt bountifully with thee. ⁸For thou hast delivered my soul from death, mine eyes from tears, and my feet from falling."

Let's consider this man. It is pretty serious when the sorrows of death surround you. It is serious when the pains of hell actually grab you. Perhaps you have been in a struggle, a place of great conflict, difficulty or distress, a place you thought you could never escape. This man was there. In fact, the drudgery (and fears) of ordinary life sometimes feel like death. It is not bad, but it is going nowhere. Perhaps dead dreams haunt you of what you could, should, or might have been, if only circumstances had been different, or you had been different. When we reflect on our own sadness and uncertainties, when we are in great distress, when we feel we have come to the end of our rope and nothing changes, when we come to the point of the sorrows of death, here is where God comes into the picture. With our awesome, real, Almighty, loving, Savior, the end of our rope is transformed by the cross and the resurrection to the beginning of our hope. The sorrows of death saturated and compassed Jesus, and the pains of hell were real as He went to Hades for us. He experienced our trouble and sorrow as if they were His very own. He took on our death and the penalties and judgment for our sins. Perhaps our problem is that we are not crying out like this man, but keeping these sins, conflicts, demons, brokenness to ourselves. Verse 4 says "Then called I upon the name of the LORD; O LORD, I beseech thee, deliver my soul." The theme of this book is deliverance, healing and restoration of the soul. Perhaps we should be crying out to the Lord, for He will set us free, free to be who He created us to be and saved us to be.

Here are the three great deliverances of Psalms 116: He has delivered my soul from death—Jesus brings salvation to the soul. The wages of sin is death, and the soul dies because of sin. But Jesus saves our souls—from the lies of hell, from confusion, from bad situations, from deception, sin, from slumber, from demons, from eternal death. Second, He delivers our eyes from tears. He protects us and takes us out of the sorrows that overwhelm others. The scripture promises that someday there will be no tears. He will wipe them away. But even before that "someday" in heaven, He can do a great work of healing, redemption, restoration, deliverance and protection now. Our lives can be one of joy and not tears. No matter how great the pain, the power of our God is greater to deliver our eyes from tears, and protect us from situations that will cause tears, and also use those tears to bring life to others. Maybe this is not what we envisioned or wanted, but there can be victory over pain. Third, He delivers our feet from falling. He will keep us out of the snares of the devil. He will "lead us not into temptation." He will deliver us from evil. He will keep us from falling into the immoral situations that destroy others, from the foolish things others do that ruin families, lives, finances, homes, and eternities. He will keep us on the paths of righteousness, which have great reward, for His name's sake.

Jesus said in Revelation 21: "7 He that overcometh shall inherit all things, and I will be His God and he shall be my son." This is the end result of our victory in this world through Christ. The victory starts on the inside of us, because the kingdom of heaven is within, and then it grows daily in our walk and openness to Him and His patterns and plans. This is not a small battle or a small victory, it is a massive battle and a massive victory, but it is well worth it, to be fully capable of inheriting all things and being a child of the Living God. Jesus died for this victory and He rose again proving that with God all things are possible. He put His blood on the mercy seat of heaven, and ever lives to make intercession to make sure that everything He has paid for with His blood will be realized by us. His blood has bought everything, our lives, our eternity, our holiness, our wholeness, our relationship with the Father, freedom from all the works of the devil, our promises and inheritance, and the freedom to be and become, instead of be damned. Because of the blood we experience this victory in totality. He gives us the Holy Spirit to lead, sanctify and empower us. He urges us not to stop short. The scripture states in Hebrews 12: "[1]Wherefore seeing we also are compassed about with so great a cloud of witnesses, let us lay aside every weight, and the sin which doth so easily beset us, and let us run with patience the race that is set before us, [2]Looking unto Jesus the author and finisher of our faith; who for the joy that was set before him endured the cross, despising the shame, and is set down at the right hand of the throne of God." So let's go ahead and take all Christ has done for us and follow Him in faith to final victory.

Now, going back to Psalms 116, how does this man repay the Lord for all His goodness? In fact, how can we ever repay Him? Here is what he says: "[12]What shall I render unto the LORD for all his benefits toward me? [13]I will take the cup of salvation, and call upon the name of the LORD." To me that means I will receive everything the Lord has to give me. I will receive the full benefits of salvation, the power of the cross, the resurrection, and the power of the ages yet to come, the inheritance and destiny He has for me on earth as it is in heaven. I will embrace my place as a child of the Living God and rest in the fullness of His love. Consider the vastness and excellence of God's grace. I actually "repay" Him by receiving everything He has to give me. I will love Him because He first loved me—when I was in trouble, when I was unlovable, so that I may walk in the land of the living and be a testimony of God's goodness, love and power. I will celebrate with the cup of salvation because He has mercifully taken the cup of suffering for me. I will call upon the Lord, because He is my God, my Fortress, my Savior, my Provider, my Bridegroom, my Healer and Deliverer, my Father and Friend and Helper, and more. So, thanks be to God. Yes, [15] Thank God for his Son—his Gift too wonderful for words. II Corinthians 9:15. That's what I will do and that's what I will continue to do—I will drink to the fullest the cup of His love, because He has done all things well, and I will live in eternal relationship with Him. Thanks be to God the Father, Son and Holy Spirit. Glory to God. The End.

APPENDIX A

PRAYER OF SALVATION

Dear Heavenly Father, I ask Jesus into my heart to be my Lord and Savior. I know I am a sinner, but I believe the blood of Jesus which He shed for me on the cross, cleanses me from all sin. I believe Jesus died for me and rose from the dead. I give you my life, Lord Jesus, and ask for Your life in return. Fill me now with the Holy Spirit. In Jesus' name. Amen.

PRAYER OF REPENTENCE

Repentance for Sins of the Heart

Dear Heavenly Father, I repent of all my sins. I repent of the rebellion against You, and rebellion in my heart, disobedience, stubbornness, pride, idolatry, jealousy, envy and bitterness. I repent of unforgiveness and holding grudges, anger and resentment towards You and others. I repent of fear, doubt, and unbelief in You and Your Word. I also repent of self-hatred and self-condemnation, as well as selfishness and self-pity. I forgive now all those who have hurt, abused, rejected, and used me. I release them to You, Lord. Cleanse my heart of all that is not of You and show me the areas where I need to be cleansed, even in events and attitudes of my childhood. Make every crooked way straight in me. I also repent of the ways I have hurt others and trespassed against them, the relationships I have broken and the heartache I have caused. I repent of not forgiving myself when I have sinned when Your Word declares I am forgiven.

Create in me a clean heart, O Lord, and renew a right spirit within me. Purge me with the blood of Jesus in my heart, and wash my heart. Psalms 51. Ignite the flame of love for You, and lead me in the paths of righteousness. Heal the wounds in my heart, and heal the wounds in other hearts I have harmed. I know You require truth in the inward parts of my soul, and I invite You to be Lord of all of me.

Repentance for Sins of the Body—More on This Later

Dear Father, forgive me, too, of the sins of my flesh, uncleanness, sexual immorality (sexual relationships outside of marriage, i.e. fornication and adultery) lust, perversion, unnatural sexual practices, alcohol and drug abuse, incest, homosexuality (lesbianism), defiling my body in any way, exposure to pornography and collecting pornographic or unclean objects, adopting a false identity.

Forgive me for physically harming other human beings in any way through physical assault, rape, or even murder. I repent of harming my own body.

I repent of abortion, or aiding in an abortion, and I release that unborn child to You.

I believe in Your Word that my body is the temple of the Holy Spirit, because I belong to You, therefore I pray that You will be Lord over my body. You say in Your Word that if we confess our sins You are faithful and just to forgive us our sins and cleanse us from all unrighteousness. I John 1:9. Cleanse me now Lord, my heart, my body, my mouth, my eyes. I break all ungodly soul ties with those whom I have committed such sins, or who have committed such sins against me. I cast out now all demons operating in the area of (name the sin i.e. lust, homosexuality, pornography etc.) Fill the temple of my body with Your Spirit.

Repentance for Sins of My Mouth

Dear Heavenly Father, I ask Your forgiveness for the words I have spoken in blasphemy against God, swearing, cursing You, myself, or others, speaking unclean things, foul language, lying, gossip, slandering others, prideful boasting, occult curses or incantations. I bind any unclean spirit (address directly, for example, lying spirits, spirits of blasphemy etc.) that may use my mouth for their work, and command them to leave me. Cleanse my mouth of all unclean activities. I pray that it may speak words in line with Your will. Help me not to tear down with my mouth those You have given me to love.

"May the words of my mouth and the meditation of my heart be acceptable unto You, O Lord, my strength, and my Redeemer." Psalms 19:14.

Repentance for Sins with Money and Possessions

Dear Heavenly Father, I repent of using the money in my possession in wasteful and foolish ways. Help me to be a good steward of all that has been given to me. I repent of using my money for sinful activities, for robbing You by not trusting Your Word to give into Your kingdom, for fraudulent activities regarding my money or the money of others and for the theft of money or objects from others. Forgive me Lord for not tithing or giving when You asked me to give. You say in Your Word not to defraud our "neighbor," Leviticus 19:13, and "thou shalt not steal," Exodus 20:15. Forgive me for such injustice and sin. I forgive all those who have stolen from me and defrauded me. I repent for my family line for such sins, ask forgiveness, and I break in the name of Jesus every family line curse through the generations that has bent me in this way and has also caused me to bear the penalties for such previous sins. I ask to be released from any judgments in my family line that have come on me or my children due to fraud, theft, wastefulness, and other acts of disobedience regarding money, in Jesus' name. I also ask You for Your guidance and direction on the use of all that I have.

Repentance for Sins in Spiritual Matters

Dear Heavenly Father, I repent of spiritual adultery, that is supernatural experiences away from You, such as astrology, fortune telling, palm reading, tea-leaf reading, séances, crystal balls, tarot cards, seeking psychics, mediums, engaging in voodoo, Santeria, out-of-body experiences, witchcraft, magic or channeling, hypnosis, or any belief in reincarnation, Ouija boards, praying to idols and other such satanic and occult activities. I repent of these sins, and I also command the demons that entered me as I engaged in these sins to leave me. I renounce all material I have read in these fields, and I will destroy such books and materials in my possession and will not access the same in any way. I renounce every cult that denies the blood of Jesus, every philosophy that denies the divinity of Christ. I break in the name of Jesus Christ, all psychic heredity and any demonic hold upon my family as a result of the disobedience of my ancestors. I cast out every familiar spirit that draws me into such practices. I break every curse on me for engaging in any of the above practices or any psychic, demonic, or satanic prayers for or against me, any words of curse spoken over me, incantations, or fortunes, or other such spoken words. I also break any bonds of physical or mental illness in Jesus' name. I renounce every evil spirit that binds or torments men and I call upon the Lord Jesus to set me free.

****

I ask Your forgiveness, Lord, for the above sins, and I also forgive myself. I ask You Lord to apply the blood of the cross to every area of my spirit, soul and body. Restore my soul. In Jesus' name. Amen.

****

You may need further prayers of deliverance to get set free of demonic strongholds in areas of repeated sin or sinful patterns. Sometimes these particular sinful patterns run through the generations. Exodus 20:5 states that the iniquities of the fathers are visited on the children to the third and fourth generation of those who hate me (God). In that case a prayer of repentance for the family line, casting out the spirit, and breaking the family line pattern and curse is valuable. Again, as I stated earlier about the revelation of Apostle Robert Henderson, we address judgments against us in the courtrooms of heaven. These judgments due to sin in the bloodline may be hindering the release of God's blessings, healing, deliverance and destiny for our lives. Therefore, repent on behalf of your bloodline and anyone in your bloodline who did X, Y, Z sin, and ask that the judgments be released against you (and your family) by the blood of Jesus. After all Jesus took all these judgments on the cross, and He sets us free from the curse of the law. He is our Advocate in heaven. Evil spirits are only granted access to a person because someone somewhere opened the door through disobedience (even if it was not you). God wants to pluck out the plants in us that he has not planted and therefore insure that a crop grows in us of righteousness and life, and that we grow in the image of his son, Jesus.

Also, when we have engaged in sin with another person, or we have been victimized, controlled, or abused by another, it is valuable to break all ungodly soul ties with that person so that the connection in the spirit is broken and you can be free to be the person God created you to be.

Freedom in God is a process, but reaps great rewards. As Paul writes: "Godliness is profitable unto all things, having promise of the life that now is, and of that which is to come." 1 Timothy 4:8. And, "But we all, with open face beholding as in a glass the glory of the Lord, are changed into the same image from glory to glory, even as by the Spirit of the Lord." II Corinthians 3:18.

PRAYER TO RECEIVE THE BAPTISM OF THE HOLY SPIRIT

Dear Heavenly Father, You say in Your Word that we will receive power when the Holy Spirit is come upon us, and that the Holy Spirit is a gift for all believers. You say that Jesus is the Baptizer in the Holy Spirit. Now, Lord Jesus, I ask You to baptize me in the Holy Spirit with evidence of speaking in tongues, that is, a new heavenly language to communicate with You. Fill me with the gifts of the Holy Spirit, so I may do Your will on earth as it is in heaven.

****

Jesus wants us to cleanse the temple of God, (us), so we may be filled with the glory of God, and the power of the Holy Spirit. He calls us be in covenant (agreement) with Him, thereby receiving the blessings promised by the Father.

Repentance is not simply a prayer of our mouths, but an attitude of our hearts by which our actions will follow i.e. fruits of repentance. To repent means to "turn away". Our Heavenly Father wants us to turn away from that which is worthless, destructive and sinful, so we can be emptied and released to receive His miraculous and abundant life. Jesus' first message was "Repent, for the kingdom of heaven is at hand." The kingdom of heaven truly is at hand, waiting to enter our hearts to strengthen, bless, restore, and make our lives new. Bring fruits of repentance, in other words, our actions should show evidence of repentance.

****

I ask Your forgiveness Lord for the above sins, and I also forgive myself. I ask You Lord to apply the blood of the cross to every area of my spirit, soul and body. Restore my soul. In Jesus' name. Amen.

APPENDIX B

UNCLEAN SPIRITS MENTIONED IN THE BIBLE

1. Spirit of antichrist. I John 4:3. In the Greek, an opponent of the Messiah. "Anti" means opposite, instead of contrast, or substitution of Christ, the Anointed One. Characteristics: Will not confess the Lordship of Jesus Christ, and that Jesus has come in the flesh as the Savior of the world. Also, the spirit tries to break the connections between the Father and the Son and the Son and the Holy Spirit and strip the anointing of the Holy Spirit off the earth. See especially I John Chapter 2. Antichrist will be a person ruling on earth in a false Satanic trinity. See Revelation 13 and 14.

2. Spirit of bondage. Romans 8:15. Originates from the Greek, meaning slavery, or to be a slave or be in bondage, do service. Also originates from subjection or subservient, to bind, be in bonds, knit, tie, and wind. Characteristics: It leads to fear, and lack of understanding of the Father/Son relationship in God. Romans 8:15.

3. Spirit of deep sleep. Isaiah 29:10-12, or slumber, Romans 11:8. In the Greek, it means lethargy, trance, and originates from stun, stupefy, cast into a dead sleep. Characteristics: Spiritual eyes closed, lack of prophecy, no scriptural revelation.

4. Spirit of divination. Acts 16:16-18. In the Greek, a python, inspiration, soothsaying. Characteristics: Opposes the truth, channeling for money, grievous.

5. Spirit of error. I John 4:6. In the Greek, fraudulence, straying from orthodoxy or piety, deceit, delusion, feminine of seducing. Characteristics: Not of God and will not hear the truth.

6. Evil spirit. I Samuel 16:14, Judges 9:23, Acts 19:12. In the Greek, hurtful, degenerate from original virtue, calamity, derelict, guilt, lewd. In the Hebrew, bad, adversary, affliction, calamity, displeased, distress, grief, harm, heavy, hurtful, misery, noisome, sad, sorrow, trouble, vex. Characteristics: Violence, insanity, persecuting.

7. Familiar spirit. I Samuel 28:7, Isaiah 29:4. In the Hebrew, familiar friend. Characteristics: Familiar with the identity, past, and characteristics of the people afflicted by it. Familiar spirits are used to supposedly to contact the dead. They are used by mediums to obtain information, and they transmit information.

8. Spirit of fear. II Timothy 1:7. In the Greek, timidity, dread, faithless. Characteristics: Fear of using spiritual gifts, dread.

9. Foul spirit. Mark 9:25. In the Greek, impure morally, lewd, unclean, dumb and deaf. Characteristics: Self-destructive behavior, lewd and unclean, same as described in Greek.

10. Spirit of heaviness. Isaiah 61:3. In the Hebrew, feeble, obscure, darkish, grow dim, smoking, weak, despondent, fail, faint. Characteristics: Lack of praise, oppression and depression.

11. Spirit of infirmity. Luke 13:11. In the Greek, feebleness of body or mind, malady, frailty, disease, sickness, weakness, without strength, or impotent. Characteristics: Same.

12. Spirit of jealousy. Numbers 5:30. In the Hebrew, envy, zeal, moved to provoke. Characteristic: Suspicion.

13. Lying spirit. II Chronicles 18:21. In the Hebrew, untruth, sham, deceit, falsehood, cheat, be untrue. Characteristics: Same as described and entice, hides hatred.

14. Perverse spirit. Isaiah 19.14. In the Hebrew, perversity, do amiss, make crooked, trouble, or do wrong. Characteristics: Error, afraid, fear, same as described.

15. Seducing spirit. I Timothy 4:1. In the Greek, roving, as a tramp or an imposter, deceiver. Characteristics: Draw those away from the faith.

16. Unclean spirit. Mark 5:8. Greek, same as foul spirit. General term for spirits not of God.

17. Spirit of whoredom. Hosea 4:12. In the Hebrew, adultery, idolatry, from wanton, commit adultery, usually of the female, harlotry. Characteristics: Unfaithfulness to God and husband, come out from under authority, prostitution.

Please note that there are spirits attached to names, persons and entities, as well, such as Baal, Moloch, Jezebel, Ahab, Leviathan, Legion, Ashtoreth, Delilah, Apollyon, etc. Spirits such as Jezebel, Baal, Moloch, and Leviathan, can be ruling spirits in nations. We also see in the book of Daniel, the Prince of Persia and the Prince of Greece. These are principalities over nations.

APPENDIX C

PRAYER TO BREAK PATTERNS OF SIN IN FAMILY AND BREAK FAMILY LINE CURSES

Dear Heavenly Father, I want patterns of sins in my family line to end—beginning with ME. I desire to be free in You and without guilt, or shame or condemnation of the past. I desire to be set free from the curses coming down on me because of the sins of the generations before me and because of the sins I have committed.

I now, therefore, break in the name of the Lord Jesus Christ, the patterns of these sins in my family line, and the curses that my family and myself have reaped and the judgments that have come on us because of these sins, and ask for forgiveness for myself—if I have committed any of these sins, and repent for the generations— fathers, mothers, grandparents, and other relatives on both sides of my family that went before me for the following sins. I break and release myself from all evil inheritance of the curses associated with these sins and the judgments that have come upon us because of these sins and I break the patterns of these sins that I have inherited or committed:

Rebellion, disobedience, pride, stubbornness, idolatry, jealousy, envy and bitterness. Anger, resentment towards You and others.

Fear, doubt, unbelief in You and Your word. Rejection of the Father, Son (Jesus Christ) or Holy Spirit.

Self-hatred, hatred of others, self-pity, self-condemnation, self-ishness and prejudice.

Rejection of myself and others, including rejection of my gender identity given at birth.

Abuse and disrespect of self, children, spouse, parents, physical abuse, sexual abuse, emotional abuse, verbal abuse, drug abuse, alcohol abuse, molestation of children. Family breakup through divorce, adultery, fornication and sexual sins, and irresponsibility.

Sexual immorality: fornication (sex outside of heterosexual marriage), adultery, incest, homosexuality, lesbianism, bestiality, exposure to pornography or unclean objects, self-abuse. Set me free from family line patterns of having children outside of marriage, though I believe that God loves every child born into the world.

Physical assault, violence, murder, rape, abortion, assisting in an abortion.

Blasphemy against God or cursing others, lying, swearing, gossip, slander, prideful boasting, occult curses.

Robbing God by not giving of my money, not tithing, disobeying the Lord with regard to money. Theft, robbery, break-in, destroying other people's property wasting money and resources, selfishness with money and possessions.

I repent for not trusting God to provide for me and not believing God can use the abilities He has given me and I break this generational curse of dependency.

I repent (as applicable) for witchcraft, sorcery, fortune telling, astrology, palm reading, tea-leaf reading, séances, crystal balls, tarot cards, psychic experiences, seeking mediums, engaging in voodoo, Santeria, out-of-body experiences, magic, channeling, hypnosis, belief in reincarnation, Ouija boards, praying to idols, animal or human sacrifices, and other satanic or occult activities; witchcraft practices coming from any area of the world—Europe, Asia, Africa, South America, Central America, Mexico, North America, Australia, the islands of the sea, and any other place. I repent and ask release from the sins and curses of the witchcraft or sorcery practices of the generations before me of any type going back to my ancestors.

Release me from any curses on me or my family because of belief in a religion that does not acknowledge Jesus Christ as the only begotten Son of God Who paid for our redemption from sin through His own blood, that denies the resurrection of Jesus Christ, or dethrones Father God, or the Holy Spirit. (You may be specific here if you have been involved in a cult.)

Lord, I ask you to release me from the patterns of the above sins and the curses of and from these sins. I go now to the courts of heaven by the blood of Jesus, to be released from the judgments from these sins upon me and my family.

I ask you Lord to break the curses of poverty, loss, family breakdown, mental and emotional confusion, hereditary sickness, barrenness, unnatural deaths, suicides and being accident-prone, and any type of victimization on my life.

Lord, pull out the root of these sins and curses, and fill me with your life and love. Make me a new creature in all areas. I ask you Lord to make me a blessing to others, and instead of being disobedient I ask to be made into an obedient son/daughter of Your love. I pray this in the name of the Lord Jesus Christ.

(If there are specific sins that seem to be repeated in your life, repent for yourself, break the pattern of these sins through the generations and the curses/judgments of these sins, and ask the Lord to fill in the empty spaces and recreate you in his image.)

PRAYER FOR BREAKING CONTROL AND VICTIMIZATION

Dear Heavenly Father, I have been a victim of control by other people and desire to be free. I break in the name of Jesus Christ all evil power, possession and control of (name person-this can be a relative, friend, enemy, person in authority, or any other person) over me, and every ungodly soul tie between me and (name person) in the area of (sexual, emotional, mental or physical abuse [name anything else]). I forgive those who have trespassed against me, and ask to be forgiven for hatred, anger, or resentment I might have. Restore my soul and return to me all of my soul tied to any person in an ungodly way. Heal my heart.

Dear Heavenly Father, I declare myself a victor in Christ Jesus, and more than a conqueror, as the Bible says. I break curses over myself and my family and the generations before me of victimization and oppression, the effects of injustice and slavery, cruelty and prejudice, poverty and lack. I claim my inheritance in Christ Jesus.

I also, Lord, do not want to be in bondage to sin, but a victor over it, and I ask you to fill me with the Holy Spirit, so I may live a holy life. I pray this and declare this in the name of Jesus Christ.

FOR THOSE ETHNIC AND RELIGIOUS GROUPS WHO HAVE BEEN GREATLY PERSECUTED

Please note here many ethnic/religious groups have been victims of horrible crimes—genocide, mass murder. These traumatic experiences have an effect on future generations. The resulting sadness, oppression, shame, need to be addressed and healed by the Holy Spirit. This would include forgiveness of the perpetrators and leaving them to God.

APPENDIX D

PRAYER FOR BREAKING SOUL TIES

I break in the name of Jesus all evil power, possession and control of (name person) over me, and every ungodly soul tie between men and (name person) in the area of (drug use, sexual activities, abuse—whatever else the Lord gives you). Dear Lord, restore my soul and return to me all of my soul tied to that person in an ungodly way.

As I wrote earlier: The ungodly covenants of joining a gang or occult organization, can be controlling for life. I will also include religious systems that are not based on the word of God. In such a case, break the covenant (even blood covenant) with that gang or group, and enter into the blood covenant with the Lord Jesus Christ.

Pray this prayer: I break this blood covenant now with XXX in the name of Jesus Christ, and I join myself to Jesus Christ by covenant through the blood He shed on the cross. I break every covenant with death. I break every covenant with [such and such] person or group that was not of you. I break all my vows and covenants with XXX organization. In Jesus' name.

Appendix E

RENUNCIATION OF SEXUAL SINS
PRAYERS FOR FREEDOM FROM SEXUAL SIN
PRAYERS TO BREAK UNGODLY SOUL TIES
PRAYERS TO BREAK CURSES OF SEXUAL SIN

A. Repentance/Renouncing/Breaking Curses

Dear Heavenly Father, I repent on behalf of myself and the generations before me, on my mother's side of the family, and on my father's side of the family, for all sexual sin, including, fornication, adultery, pornography, homosexuality, lesbianism—[ADD OTHERS as necessary, such as rape, incest, prostitution, ritual sex] and for all patterns of sexual sin, multiple marriages and generations of fornication.

I command all spirits of fornication, uncleanness, homosexuality, lesbianism, pornography, adultery [ADD OTHERS] [possibly false identity, if you are pretending to be a male or female] to leave me. [YOU CAN COMMAND MALE OR FEMALE SPIRITS TO LEAVE—IF THAT IS NOT YOUR TRUE SEXUAL/GENDER IDENTITY.]

I break all ungodly soul ties and ungodly covenants with those whom I have had sexual relations with, outside of marriage as defined in the Bible. [YOU CAN NAME THESE PEOPLE, AND EXPLICITLY BREAK TIES WITH THEM IF YOU KNOW THEIR NAMES. IF NOT, JUST BREAK ALL SEXUAL ENCOUNTERS OUTSIDE OF MARRIAGE.]

Lord, I ask you to return to me all fragments of my soul that have been torn away by ungodly soul ties in sexual relationships outside of marriage and I command any part of the souls of other people to leave me.

I repent of and renounce ungodly forms of sex such as homosexual (including lesbian) practices, fetishes, sadomasochism, and

MANY more. I break ties with these practices, and renounce them.

Forgive [me or the generations before me] for having families outside of marriage. Lord, I ask you to break generational patterns and curses of illegitimacy, and I consecrate my children to you.

Release me and cleanse me from the shame that pulls down my life and heart.

B. Forgiveness and Breaking of Soul Ties--Molestation, Rape, Abuse

I forgive those [NAME THESE PEOPLE] who have sexually used me and molested me, raped, and abused me. I break all ungodly soul ties with those who have used me, molested me, raped or abused me.

Dear Lord, cleanse me from fear, grief, heartache, self-hatred, hatred, anger, rage. hatred of (men/women). I forgive myself for being used, and I forgive my (mother/father/caregiver) for not protecting me.

I repent for all sins in the family line, on my mother's side of the family, and my father's side of the family, of rape, incest, sexual abuse, and I ask You, Lord, to break these curses in my family line, and set me free from associated judgments against me and my family in the name of Jesus.

I command unclean spirits of molestation, rape, abuse, grief, rejection, incest, abandonment, heartache, death, perversion, to leave me.

Release me and cleanse me from the shame that pulls down my life and heart.

C. Especially for African Americans

I forgive those who separated and destroyed families as a result of slavery. I forgive and release them, and I ask you Lord to break the curse of separation, divorce, and detachment over my family. I forgive those who used and abused my slave ancestors sexually, verbally, emotionally, mentally, and economically, and I break the curses of such captivity and oppression.

D. For Those Who Have Engaged in Homosexuality/Lesbianism

Dear Heavenly Father, I repent of (homosexuality/lesbianism). I know it is a sin. I renounce these practices, and I ask you Lord to remake my life in the image of your Son. Give me an identity in You. I forgive those who introduced me to homosexual practices, or molested me.

I ask You, Lord, to break generational curses of homosexuality and lesbianism in my life, and I repent on behalf of my family, on my mother's side of the family, and my father's side of the family, for such sins.

I command all unclean, perverse, homosexual (or lesbian) spirits to leave me.

I break every ungodly soul tie with those persons with whom I have had a homosexual/lesbian relationship, including pornography in these areas. I renounce any false marriage or partnership.

I ask You, Lord, to rise up in me and give me strength to walk as Your Son walked. Release me and cleanse me from the shame that pulls down my life and heart.

Work in my life that I may reclaim my true self according to the pattern of the word of God. Break down the barriers I have had in my heart to my (father or mother, men or women). I forgive my same sex parent for abandoning, neglecting or abusing me, and not releasing to me my true identity.

[For those who have engaged in homosexuality or lesbianism, it is valuable to receive deliverance, mind renewal, counselling, and prayers for inner healing.]

E. Transgenders and Transsexuals

[For those who have changed their bodily identity, or want to change gender or act like another gender, it is valuable to repent of self-hatred, mutilation, deception, pretending to be someone else, and also cast out the false male or female spirit, some of which may have a personal female or male name, and any spirit of confusion.

Ask the Lord to reorder and change body chemistry to what is designed for a male or female.]

Dear Heavenly Father, I repent for degrading and rejecting my identity, and seeking to be a woman (if I am a man) or seeking to be a man (if I am a woman). I forgive those who may have caused me to hate myself, and detach from my true identity, and I repent and forgive myself, for self-hatred and self-rejection and rebellion against my Creator.

I renounce all such sin, and repent of such sin in my own life, and I ask you to break all generational curses in the area of fornication, adultery, pornography, homosexuality, lesbianism, rape, incest, prostitution, transgendered lifestyles [NAME OTHERS] in my life.

I repent and renounce dressing like a member of the opposite sex, and I ask forgiveness for wanting to change my identity. Take away my attraction to clothes of the opposite sex, and help me to be content with who I am. Show me the root of this so I may be free.

I repent for debasing and degrading my body, and rejecting the true identity that you have given me. I repent for taking hormones and mutilating my body in trying to change my sexual identity. I repent of self-hatred, and self-rejection, and taking on the identity of a gender other than what I was created to be. I renounce all (female or male) spirits. I ask you to break every ungodly soul tie with those I have had sex. I renounce any false marriage or partnership.

I forgive those who caused me to hate or reject myself.

I forgive those who have bought, misled, prostituted, or harmed me.

Lord, take me back to my true identity and make me whole. Release me and cleanse me from the shame that pulls down my life and heart. Take away the barriers in my heart that have stopped me from realizing my true identity and loving myself.

F. Repentance for Abortion

Dear Heavenly Father, I am sorry for aborting my child (or agreeing to the abortion of my child, if you are the father). I know this is the sin of murder, and I am sorry.

I release my child to You, knowing that we will be united one day.

I trust you to heal my life, and fill in the gap of emptiness. I repent for the generations before me, on my mother's side of the family, and my father's side of the family, for the sin of abortion, and I break every curse of abortion over my life. Release me from the judgments on my life or family line because of abortion.

I repent in assisting with an abortion, or encouraging or compelling a woman to have an abortion.

G. Additional Actions

These prayers are just a starting point and there are many more steps in the delivering and healing process, but they open the door for the Lord to start bringing His life to spirit, soul and body.

OTHER ACTIONS YOU CAN TAKE: Destroy all sexual literature in your home. Do not access sexually related websites and apps. Get rid of sexually explicit materials. Throw them away. THESE ATTRACT DEMONIC SPIRITS, AND BRING OPPRESSION AND HEAVINESS AND LUST INTO YOUR OWN HOUSE. Throw away sexual objects, and consider getting rid of gifts, clothes, and objects from former sexual partners.

APPENDIX F

WARFARE PRAYERS
How to Protect You, Your Family, and Loved Ones

Hosea 4:6 says, "My people are destroyed for a lack of knowledge." God has given us knowledge in His word as to how to defeat the enemy, but we must be aware of that knowledge and use it. Let us not be ignorant of the devices of the enemy, nor of the authority we have in Christ Jesus to gain victory over Satan and release the plan and protection of God in our lives through the blood of Jesus.

1. STEP ONE: Pray each day for yourself and loved ones, every day, no matter what. You may be standing in the gap for them between life and death. Place them (and yourself) under the blood of Jesus, and ask God to release angels to protect them. FOR EXAMPLE, YOU CAN PRAY AS FOLLOWS.

Dear Heavenly Father, I pray for (name loved ones), cover them with the blood of Jesus and surround, encamp, and protect them with angels.

2. STEP TWO: In addition to our everyday prayers be sensitive to the Holy Spirit—the Lord may be telling you of special times in which we are to pray. Actually we are to pray without ceasing. This means be in an attitude of prayer and relationship with God. Jesus ever lives to make intercession and to some extent, so do we by our alertness in the spirit and having a life attitude of standing in the gap.

Be Spirit-filled. Receive the baptism of the Holy Spirit with the evidence of speaking in tongues. Acts 1:8. PRAY IN TONGUES. Praying in tongues not only builds up your faith, (Jude v. 20), but gives you insight into the spirit world. God may show you something to save your life.

3. STEP THREE: Take authority over all principalities, powers, rulers of the darkness of this world etc. by means of BINDING AND

LOOSING PRAYERS. <u>Break enemy assignments against you.</u>

Jesus said: "And I give you the keys of the kingdom of heaven, and whatever you bind on earth will be bound in heaven, and whatever you loose on earth will be loosed in heaven." Matthew 16:19.

Paul wrote: "For we wrestle not against flesh and blood, but Against principalities, against powers, against the rulers of the darkness of this age, against spiritual hosts of wickedness in the heavenly places." Ephesians 6:12.

"For the weapons of our warfare is not carnal (against flesh), but mighty in God for pulling down of strongholds." II Corinthians 10:4

HOW TO WE DO PUT THIS ALL TOGETHER AND PRAY?

In the name of the Lord Jesus Christ, I take authority over all principalities, powers, rulers of the darkness of this world, spiritual wickedness in high places, satanic angels, and demonic hosts and all designs and assignments of the enemy operating in the area of (name realm of demonic stronghold, such as witchcraft, drug and alcohol use, gang warfare, violence, anger, family breakup, sexual immorality, perversion, death, destruction, antichrist, occult activities, strife, unbelief, rebellion, pride, etc. in and over--name yourself, relatives, etc.).

THE NEXT STEPS HAVE TO DO WITH YOUR LIFE

4. STEP FOUR: Be Obedient to God.

II Corinthians 10:4 and 6 says "For the weapons of our warfare are not carnal but might in God, for pulling down strongholds--and being ready to punish all disobedience <u>when your obedience is fulfilled</u>."

Obedience gives power in the spirit. When we walk in obedience the flow of God's love and power works to fulfill that obedient walk.

When we rebel, we only invite demons to harass us. The Bible says that the way of the transgressor is hard. Proverbs 13:15.

5. STEP FIVE: Live a Holy Life.

Confess all known sin. Repent of it. Get it out of your life. Ask God to cleanse you, for we are promised, that "if we confess our sin He is faithful and just to forgive us of your sin and cleanse us from all unrighteousness." I John 1:9. Get set free from ungodly relationships, associations, addictions and attachments. (See prayer to break ungodly soul ties).

Holiness is not wearing a white dress or carrying a Bible. Holiness is an inner purity through repentance and forgiveness of sins, and the cleansing, delivering work of the Holy Spirit and the blood of Jesus in our lives. It will result in a worshipful attitude towards God, obedience, and childlike trust in God that enables power in the Spirit to operate in our lives. The Bible says that without holiness, no man can see God. Hebrews 12:14. Therefore, the depth of our relationship with God depends on it.

And without holiness, the devil has access to you. Every area of sin is a door for demonic attack and oppression. Your authority will be reduced in the spiritual realm

6. STEP SIX: Be Set Free.

Along with living a holy life, be delivered and healed from hurts, wounds, brokenness, rejection, captivity on the inside. Then the Spirit of God will rise up big in you, instead of being hindered by demonic activity, and wounds that have not been healed. YOU CANNOT RUN THE RACE IF YOUR FEET ARE TIED AND YOUR LEGS BROKEN.

Break curses and family line patterns of sin in every area of your life. When the enemy has no hold on you, then you can take a firm stand against him. Jesus said "for the ruler of this world is coming and he has nothing in me." (See prayers to break curses.)

7. STEP SEVEN: Be in Constant Relationship with God.

He will deliver you and guide you away from evil. The Holy

Spirit is the Spirit of Truth who will show you the way you are to go. Your integrity and honesty will keep you out of the way of evil. Ask the Lord to guide your steps daily. Put on the whole armor of God as described in Ephesians 6:14-17, and "pray always with all prayer," v. 18. In putting on the armor of God, you may say out loud— "I now put on the breastplate of righteousness, the shield of faith, my loins are girt about with truth, my feet shod with the preparation of the gospel of peace, I carry the sword of the Spirit, and have the shield of faith and helmet of salvation." Learn what these mean.

WHAT YOU CAN DO IN YOUR HOME AND PROPERTY

8. STEP EIGHT: Anoint Your Home with Oil.

Go through your house, pray over it and anoint it with oil. What does this mean and how do you do this? To anoint something with oil is to declare it holy, dedicated to God, and cleansed. To anoint with oil, take a little oil—cooking oil, olive oil, put it in a separate container and declare it holy unto God in the name of the Lord Jesus Christ. Then put a little bit of it on your finger or hand and touch the walls of your home in every room, your bed, your furniture. Break curses over the house or apartment, the property, and the objects in it, commanding every unclean spirit to leave in the name of Jesus. Break demonic strongholds from former owners or residents. For example, you may know that a crime was committed at your apartment. Anoint the apartment with oil. Take authority over every spirit of violence there, and command it to leave. Ask that your home be covered with the blood of Jesus, and ask the Holy Spirit to abide there. Command evil spirits of sexual immorality or drug use or whatever might be there – strife, suicide, anger, etc. – to leave, and bind the spirits up, and command them to go into the dry places as the scripture tells us. If you have a yard, you can go out in the yard and anoint it with oil, pouring oil onto the property and declaring it holy to the Lord, commanding unclean spirits to leave, and breaking curses over the land.

9. STEP NINE: Rid Your Home of Unclean Objects.

Get rid of, destroy, trash all ungodly objects in your possession such as pornography, drug paraphernalia, sexual objects, idols, literature on the occult or from false religions, music that is displeasing to God. Likewise do not access pornographic websites, for example. Then the Lord will want to dwell there. These items and spiritual doorways attract demons. Deuteronomy 7:26 says: "Nor shall you bring an abomination into your house, lest you be doomed to destruction like it. You shall utterly detest it and utterly abhor it, for it is an accursed thing."

10. STEP TEN: Worship God.

The Lord inhabits the praises of His people, and our praises still the enemy. Psalms 22:3 and Psalms 2:2. As you are in an attitude of praise and worship, the Spirit of the Lord will increase in you and your circumstances. The enemy is pushed out by such an environment and the presence and power of God increases.

APPENDIX G

Understanding and Healing the Mother Wound

Written by Alfred C.W. Davis[3]

We all come into the world needing the tender presence of a mother's touch, nurture, care and love. In fact, the mother's influence begins when we are in the womb. The absence of this mother love is a wound that is created in three ways:

1. Mother is separated from the child through:
    1. illness of the mother
    2. mother's death
    3. divorce.

2. Child is separated from the mother through:
    1. illness of the child
    2. incubator/hospitalization
    3. adoption.

3. Unhappy relationship with mother through:
    1. neglect
    2. abuse
    3. mother's mental and emotional distress
    4. attempted abortion.

When this most important attachment is traumatically interrupted, there is emotional pain that produces consequences within the individual. The effect of the wounding includes:

- Feelings of abandonment and dread of aloneness
- Loss of self and sense of being

---

3   This article is printed and distributed with permission of Alfred C.W. Davis, www.lovehealstv.com

- Powerful hunger for feminine touch that can be eroticized
- Emotional dependencies
- Possible gender confusion, fear and insecurity.

There are two main responses to a mother wound that affect one's ability to achieve healthy friendships and healthy married love:

1. Emotional detachment – This defensive response to the breakdown in the mother's love causes a detachment from the mother. The legitimate need for love from the mother is repressed, leaving the child hungry but unable to secure relationships because of the emotional shutdown. The person fears the pain of attachment and therefore builds protective walls to hide behind.

2. Emotional dependency – In this response, the person strives endlessly to fill the void which often turns into co-dependency with grasping, clutching and infantile tendencies. This striving for attachment is based in low self-confidence, fear, insecurity and often confusion about self-worth.

Implications for women

- internalize a low view of women
- addictive, emotional and romantic dependencies
- infantile desire for union with women
- sexual confusion related to touch.

Implications for men

- ambivalence towards women – need them but very wary
- fixate on feminine objects of desire to fill the deprivation of mother love
- either detach or remain in toxic grip of a sinful alliance with mother

- sexual confusion related to touch.

Other implications

- separation anxiety that leads to striving, passivity and depression
- fantasy bonding – attaching to fantasies
- fetish bonding – attaching to things, clothing, hair
- attachment to self–fantasy image of self
- emotional incest – meeting emotional needs of mother
- weak sense of identity and of being.

Addressing the mother wound

There are three steps to addressing the mother wound:

1. Invite Jesus into your initial memories and emotions
2. Release your pain to Jesus and stop living from the centre of your wounded child
3. Forgive your mother
4. Strengthen your sense of identity and knowledge of your True Self in Christ.

Inviting Jesus into the wound. "*Though my father and mother forsake me, the Lord will receive me.*" (Psalm 27:10) "*As a mother comforts her child, so I will comfort you.*" (Isaiah 66:13) Knowing that Jesus wants to heal all who are broken-hearted, invite Jesus to enter into the place of your brokenness – in the womb, at birth, early in life, wherever it happens to be.

Release your painful memories to Jesus. Ask Jesus to take away the pain in each painful memory and replace it with His love. He will creatively remove the pain (the "how" is often different for each person) and then transform the memory with His love and truth.

Forgive your mother. Choose, as an act of your free will, to forgive your mother and let go of all the resentment, bitterness and anger. Jesus' transforming love will change the perspective of the trauma and free you to accept the circumstances with grace and mercy.

Strengthen your sense of identity and knowledge of your True Self in Christ. Ask Jesus to reveal the truth about who you are. As Jesus affirms your sense of being, He provides an assurance of worth and helps you know the True Self that He created. Then, look to your success stories to see the outworking of your True Self in real life.

As you connect with Jesus' profound love for you, the need for other attachments reduces your need to be loved and allows you to look outward at loving relationships with others. Living with your new self and being open to affirmation will free you to grow in your own story instead of constantly striving to attach to your mother or the substitute for your mother.

APPENDIX H

Understanding and Healing the Father Wound

Written by Alfred C.W. Davis[4]

We all come into the world helpless, dependent and needing acceptance, to be treated as worthy, and to be blessed. The *father wound* is the absence of this love from your birth father. The wound can be caused by:

- Neglect – I am unimportant
- Absence – Divorce, separation, death
- Abuse – Mental, physical, sexual, spiritual
- Control – Oppressive domination
- Withholding – *Love, blessings and/or affirmation*, deficiencies that lead to a profound lack of self-acceptance.

The effect of a father wound is low self-esteem, a deep emotional pain inside and a performance orientation that makes us "doers" rather than "beings." While salvation makes us new creations in Christ, it does not necessarily address this wound inside. We tend to have four barriers that inhibit the healing of this wound:

- **Pride** – No will to confront or change, "I'm alright"
- **Sin** – A blocked will that neither seeks to confess sin or receive forgiveness
- **The wound itself** – Continuous emotional hurt inside
- **Lies** – Misconceptions about the Self, birth father and Father God.

Instead of going to the pain and receiving the healing we need, we tend to respond to life events by creating a misconception about our "Self."

---

4   This article is printed and distributed with permission of Alfred C.W. Davis, www.lovehealstv.com

Relationship to our birth father

When we hold a conception of our birth father as angry, violent, uncaring, indifferent, distant/withdrawn, absent/abandoning, alcoholic, condemning and/or critical, we tend to believe the following words about ourselves:

- I am unworthy
- I am stupid
- I am incompetent
- I am unloved or unlovable

As long as we accept these words *as truth*, we will experience depressed, anxious and angry lives.

Relationship to God the Father

Often a person's image of God the Father is contaminated by the personal experience he or she has with the birth father. When misconceptions about God are present (i.e. that He is angry, judgmental, unhappy with me, fearsome, legalistic, quick to punish and slow to forgive . . .) the words we tend to believe are:

- I am not good enough
- I am guilty/shameful
- I must work harder to justify myself

As long as we accept these words as truth, we will seek to perform and prove our worth through perfectionism and materialism, or seek addictions to cover up the pain.

Addressing the Father Wound

There are four steps to addressing the father wound:

1. Understanding the heart of God
2. Inviting Jesus into the wounds created by the birth father
3. Accepting the truth about one's Self as a child of God
4. The heart of God.

As seen in the Prodigal Son story:
- we are free to choose our own path
- the father waits patiently for us to return to Him
- when we return, He accepts us unconditionally
- He runs to accept and embrace us
- He values us by celebrating God's provision for salvation
- He loves us first
- we are His beloved creation
- He offers salvation for our sin
- He wants a relationship with us.

Jesus as the Wounded Healer:
- He was tempted by Satan to know our temptations
- He experienced suffering to know our suffering
- He was rejected, mocked, beaten and crucified
- He fully understands our pain and wants to help
- 1 Peter 2:24 "By His wounds you have been healed."

Jesus Heals:
- when invited into memories, He comes
- when He comes into memories, my clients describe Him as gentle, kind, caring, loving, warm, friendly, hugging, accepting and healing.

When you understand His love:
- confess to Him the misconception you have had
- receive His forgiveness
- receive His love.

Invite Jesus into the wounds created by your birth father

Do inner healing for the memories:
- invite Jesus into the specific memories

- understand the words that you accepted at the time
- ask Jesus to reveal His truth to you
- receive His truth about who you are.

Choose to forgive your birth father:
- for hurtful words
- for hurtful actions
- for not loving you
- for not blessing you
- for affecting your image of God the Father

Accept yourself as a child of God. Receive the words of truth:
- I am accepted
- I am chosen
- I am loved
- I am God's creation
- I am precious in His sight
- I am forgiven
- I have been redeemed
- I will never be left or forsaken
- I have an eternal inheritance
- nothing can separate me from the love of God.

As you understand the truth about God's love and come to know your True Self in Christ, it will free you to let go of the pain and forgive your birth father. This new perspective created in you will now enable you to see your birth father through different eyes, and allow you to live in freedom.

www.ingramcontent.com/pod-product-compliance
Lightning Source LLC
LaVergne TN
LVHW051238080426
835513LV00016B/1657